*Ordinary Miracles*

# Ordinary
# Miracles

*a memoir*

LILY O'NEIL

ORDINARY MIRACLES © 2020, Lily O'Neil

All rights reserved. This book or parts thereof may not be reproduced in any form, stored in any retrieval system, or transmitted in any form by any means—electronic, mechanical, photocopy, recording, or otherwise—without prior written permission of the publisher, except as provided by United States of America copyright law. For permission requests, please contact the publisher.

Cover and eBook formatting by The Book Designers, Inc.

Cover art by Ashvin Harrison

Ebook (.ePub) ISBN: 978-1-7357850-1-1
Ebook (.Mobi) ISBN: 978-1-735780-2-8
Print Edition ISBN: 978-1-7357850-0-4

For information about special discounts available for bulk purchases, sales promotions, fund-raising, and educational needs please contact the publisher. We are committed to publishing works of quality and integrity. In that spirit, we are proud to offer this book to our readers; however, the story, the experiences, and the words are the Author's alone.

## DEDICATION

*To my family who, for good and bad,
helped make me who I am.*

*To my husband and children who, with their limitless
love and laughter, helped me learn to love who I am.*

*And to all those who dare to rise from the ashes.*

AUTHOR'S NOTE

I believe in truth and authenticity, within the pages of a memoir and beyond. However, I also believe in protecting individuals from unnecessary and unwanted attention. This story is my truth and I am telling it to the best of my ability in order to shine a light into the darkness, not to cast a spotlight on particular individuals. Therefore, I have changed the names of all the people in this book, and in some cases, I have altered identifying details to preserve anonymity.

# Preface

I began writing this memoir as a way to explain the unexplainable to my children. I wanted them to understand where—and who—they came from so they could understand themselves more fully. In order to do that, I had to understand it myself. For me, that meant I had to be able to put it into a story that could be shared.

I started at the beginning and let the events unfold on the page the way they did for me in real time, taking care to explain the historical information that colored my way of seeing things along the way. The whole time I wrote, I imagined my children, grown and curious, sitting down to read about the biggest heartaches of my life. I wanted them to understand not only the who and what of my journey, but the how and why.

I knew it was going to be a difficult endeavor, but I vastly underestimated the courage it would require to put my life on the page. I had to face my fears, my insecurities, and my own limiting beliefs. I had to force myself back in time to relive moments I'd rather forget. Then, one by one, I had to confront the hundreds of reasons *not* to tell my story. I debated and fretted and quit more times than I can count, but inevitably, an unrelenting voice would pop up in my head, urging me to keep writing. That voice inside of me needed to be heard.

    I pushed forward and somehow managed to anchor my experiences to words, something that had eluded me for years. By stringing them together, I found a way to make the unseen seen. My words breathed life into clinical words like "trauma" and "shame," reclaiming the humanity at the center of some deeply personal wounds. For the first time, my story seemed to exist beyond the confines of my being, and I felt free.

    Seeing my journey in black and white, I realized that by writing my own unique story, I'd written a story familiar to millions of others buried in the ashes of painful pasts. I'd written a story about rising from those ashes, a feat I once believed impossible. I knew then that my story, my truth, had to be shared beyond the boundaries of my own family. The only problem was the idea of speaking up filled me with intensely debilitating shame, the kind that demanded I remain invisible and silent.

    Telling the truth can be extremely difficult, and telling the truth about something as polarizing and inciting as incest feels insufferable. People don't talk about it, and when they do, they have very strong opinions and reactions that can inadvertently silence survivors. Further, those who have never endured incest, childhood sexual abuse, or childhood abuse of any kind, may never be able to understand or relate to what I've been through and how I've responded to it. I can barely grasp it myself. Being vulnerable about something so explosive is scary, especially when what you have to say may be met with disbelief and scrutiny.

My story might be hard to believe. Trauma that occurs within the intricate emotional webbing of family is complicated, which is why many people may not immediately understand my experiences. Sometimes the most painful and unforgiving transgressions are not what we expect them to be. Our reactions to them are not as predictable, either. From a different vantage point, one influenced by different life experiences and interpreted from a separate disposition, it may be hard to believe what I know to be true. That doesn't mean it isn't.

Afraid of what might happen if I lived in my truth, I've chosen to remain silent for most of my life. I've dutifully protected secrets to my own detriment. Like so many others, I've allowed myself to be diminished by my experiences. I've let my light be dimmed out of fear and shame and loyalty and love. But no more.

I now appreciate how important it is to shine my light brightly. Not only do I deserve to embody my most radiant self, I want to let my light serve as a beacon for others to follow through the darkness. As humans, we need to know that healing is possible, that we aren't alone, and that we are capable of freeing ourselves—and future generations—from what may seem like endless suffering. We need to know that others have walked a similar path and emerged victorious from their battles. We need to recognize that our voices, however small and insignificant they may seem, matter. And our stories need to be shared.

My job, as a memoirist, is to share my story with sincerity and that requires a genuine offering of all that is known. True to my calling, I have put my heart and soul on the page. I've included the events that have shaped me, as well as my subjective experience of them. Whenever possible, I've offered the facts and circumstances supporting the conclusions I've drawn for the sake of transparency. I've withheld nothing of importance on purpose. I've told my truth, the best way I can.

To the extent my story may feel incomplete, confusing, or unconventional—that's an honest reflection of me. I have missing pieces that I wish I could find and relay in this book, but I can't offer more than what I have. I'm writing from the place I am at now, fresh and perhaps a little raw from my experiences, because I believe there is value in capturing the fleeting emotion and understanding of a moment without the detached neutrality that comes with the passage of time. Much as the experience of giving birth varies greatly based upon *when* you ask the mother to recount it, insight can be gained from many different accounts.

So here is my story, my truth. The truth is I was raised by some wonderful people who did some really awful things. It impacted me in more ways than I can count, but I overcame my traumas (mostly) and refused to let them define me or those I love. My story unfolds for you, the reader, the way it unfolded for me. You have a front row seat to the emotional roller coaster I was strapped to for years and years. It's a crazy ride that may invoke a lot of feelings, but trust me, it's worth it in the end. At least it was for me.

# Ordinary Miracles

*a memoir*

We delight in the beauty of the butterfly, but rarely admit the changes it has gone through to achieve that beauty.

—*Maya Angelou*

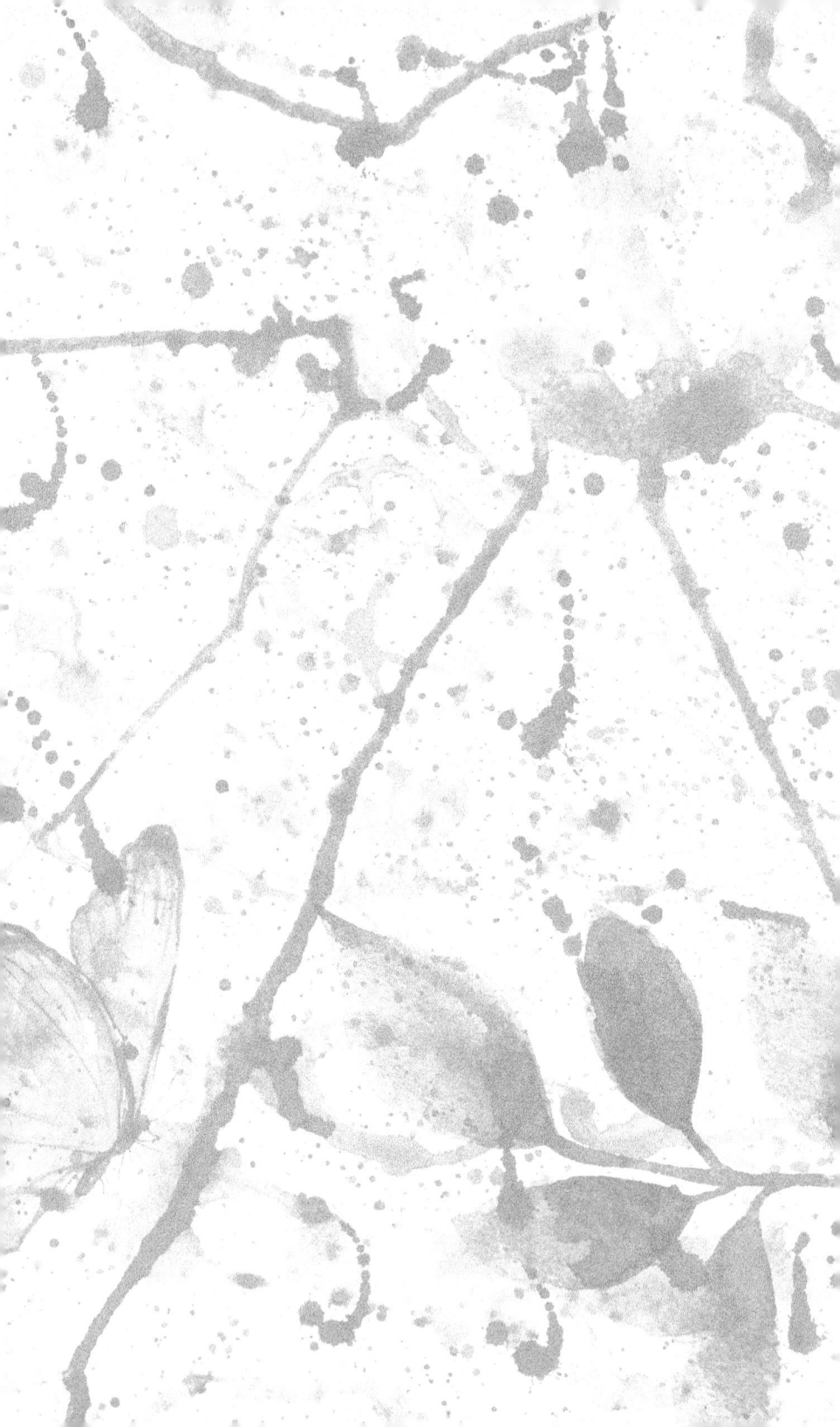

# The Egg

*The butterfly lays her eggs on a specific type of leaf. This is significant because baby caterpillars will eat only certain leaves, and since a tiny caterpillar is too small to travel to a new plant, its survival often depends on whether or not it hatches on the right leaf.*

# One

We haven't seen one another for almost a decade, yet my thoughts often drift into the treacherous terrain of what was and, more often, what might have been. It's a dangerous pastime, musing over the trajectory of two lives. There is no way to parse out the exact proportions of choice and circumstance that conspire to create our fate, yet I can't help myself. I can't help but wish for a different ending to my story, and to hers. No matter how old I get, I will always search for answers that will help me cure the brokenness.

*You only get one mother.*

She said that all the time when I was growing up. Like so many of her adages, hidden within a simple assertion of fact were layers of emotional complexity that would take years to unfold and a lifetime to appreciate. In the short term, her reminder served as a kind of insurance policy floating in the air between us, guaranteeing that I would never lose someone as irreplaceable as my own mother. She needn't have bothered reminding me; I loved her more than anything in the whole world, and deep down, I never felt that she was mine to lose in the first place. Regardless, she was right. There is some unexplainable bond between a mother and a child that cannot be severed entirely, no matter how battered it becomes. That is why my story, for good or for bad, will always intertwine with hers.

My hands are exact replicas of hers, at least they were when I studied them as a kid, even down to the curve of our white-tipped nails. I thought she was the most beautiful woman in the world, although she never truly saw it in herself. Her smile lit up her whole face and sometimes crinkled her nose. Her velvety brown eyes—"cow eyes," she called them—were warm and deep like a cup of hot cocoa on a snowy day. I sometimes think I see those eyes reflecting back at me in the mirror, but that's just wishful thinking. The hazel specks I inherited from my father diluted that rich cocoa and left me like neither her nor him.

As a child, I basked in any comparison to this marvelous woman, elated that others saw her radiant smile in me. People often said I was a mini version of her, commenting on any number of characteristics we shared in common. Our petite stature, light coloring, and rounded features made it easy enough to draw comparisons, although only in broad generalizations. It was the intangible similarities that evoked a double take. Whether by osmosis or continuous study, I emulated her bubbly mannerisms, and my words rolled off my tongue with a similar cadence. I was proud of that.

I only have a handful of old photos from my childhood, which I keep in a shoebox under the bed. They are the ones I took with me to college—before I knew what was to come. These scant images are all that I have left of my family. If I had known that these few pictures, taken in a moment of youthful haste and transience, would be all I had left to construct the faces that haunt my dreams, I would have been more selective. Even the best ones are merely flat, empty containers of the people who once inhabited them.

In the photos, my mom is smiling, the same manufactured happiness recreated in each one. No matter the circumstance, be it my First Communion or a random summer day, she is poised and beautiful, an accurate depiction of the mother I thought I had—cheerful, talkative, and overflowing with warmth and generosity. Even the backgrounds, meticulously prepared feasts and tastefully decorated mantles, exude her domestic mastery and maternal charm. Everyone loved her, including my friends who all wished to trade mothers with me. It seemed that, much like the camera lens, every person who encountered her saw the same flawless version, the version I once worshipped.

I miss her, though I don't want to, and Lord knows she has given me plenty of reasons not to. Still, on a sunny afternoon, as I watch my kids play in the yard and the sweet wildness of childhood surrounds me, I catch myself longing for her to be near. I imagine us sitting in lawn chairs with magazines in our laps, talking about new recipes and chatting about the latest celebrity gossip. If she's feeling playful, she might "make a funny" and then giggle at her own joke. If her temperament is more serious, she may look thoughtfully out at the horizon, lost in her own thoughts. And I'll hang on every word, every breath, just like I used to do when I was little.

I wish I could breathe in her familiar scent, and feel her close to me. I wish she could tell me that everything's going to be alright. I'd believe her, all too eager to pretend that I'm still a little girl, safe within her protective halo. It's a childish wish, like wanting to be a fairy princess, fully forged in my imagination. I know I've outgrown this fantasy—and her—but it's hard not to slip into such a comforting reverie.

For all I know, my mom is sitting in a lawn chair right now with another girl perched beside her, complimenting her on her latest culinary feat and listening to her bemoan the trend of blue and purple hair colors. She's probably delighting in my mom's schoolgirl laughter, soaking up her maternal doting. She'll likely go home with a Tupperware container full of leftovers and maybe a gift bag of French milled soaps, care packages once intended for me.

As my mom laughs and chatters on with the new people who have inevitably come into her life, people who see her warmth and beauty, I wonder if she ever thinks of me. It's hard to know whether or not I left a void that needed to be filled, or if my presence never took up enough space to warrant being replaced. I wonder if she misses me or if, like me, she's looking forward to the day when she realizes she no longer does.

# Two

As a child, it was the little things that mattered—the smell of my father's aftershave or my mother's floral-scented shampoo, the softness of my favorite cotton T-shirt folded neatly in my top drawer. It was the sound of Depeche Mode booming through the walls and the smell of banana bread wafting into my bedroom. And it was, more than anything else, the tradition and custom that reigned over our house during the holidays. Like a patchwork quilt, all these things—seemingly insignificant by themselves—joined together to form the security and comfort of my childhood.

I was the youngest of three, born seven and fourteen years after my older brothers, Derek and Matt. My mom referred to me as the trailer, which seemed fitting since I trailed way behind everyone in years. By the time I was born, my older brothers were on their way out of childhood, which left me as an only child of sorts.

I didn't go to preschool, a missed opportunity my mother needlessly feared would put me behind my peers. Instead, she took me to the library where we borrowed stacks of books and puppets. I would lie on her bed in the afternoon, listening to her read *Panda Cake* or *Anastasia Krupnick* or one of a million other favorites of mine, perfectly content to be at home with her. Sometimes she would take me to the high school where she and her friend would walk around the track and talk, while I played with my Barbies in the fragrant clover. Then we would go home and eat apples and tuna, or maybe some of her mouth-puckering, homemade yogurt.

When I was very little, my dad taught me how to swim. I'd climb on his back and hold my breath as he swam along the floor of our backyard pool toward the deep end for longer and longer stretches. When I couldn't breathe, I would kick his side, and after a few agonizing seconds spent believing I would die, he would swim up to the surface where I'd gasp for air. Once I got the hang of it, I spent every second I could in the pool. I lived most of my earliest years in the sunshine, wet and wild. My mom said I owned more swimsuits than shirts at one point, which was fine by me. My fair skin was permanently sun-kissed, and the skin on my nose fell off in sheets every few weeks.

My dog, Samson, joined our family when I was four. My middle brother Matt had been bitten by a dog and someone suggested getting one of our own would prevent him from developing a lifelong phobia. When a dog belonging to one of our neighbors had a litter of puppies, my parents decided to bring one home. I remember picking him out with my mom in their front yard, pointing to one of five excited jet-black balls of fur. Samson was the only one with a bright-white, star-shaped patch of fur on his chest. The moment I held his soft, wiggly body, I was in love.

Being the youngest with two older brothers out of the house all the time, I was glad for the company. Samson would hop into my inflatable boat and let me row him around our private lagoon, dodging pirates and crocodiles, then we would dry out on the grass for a bit, splitting a cold hot dog and apple juice. Samson was my best friend—my only friend for a lot of years—and we shared many memorable summers together.

As Halloween approached, my mother used to decorate the mantle with crimson- and gold-colored leaves and candles spiced with cinnamon and nutmeg. She embellished our house with porcelain ghosts, baskets filled with gourds, and an assortment of beautiful pumpkins set by the front door. Then there was Rickety Rack, the life-sized skeleton she sewed out of festive fabric and ribbons, prominently displayed in the entryway. Although there was always a bowl filled with nuts still in their shells, I was partial to the ceramic dish filled with candy corn.

I always dreamed of spending the day at the pumpkin patch, riding the tractor around the fields and scoping out the best possible pumpkin to carve. As it turned out, we usually picked up our pumpkins at the farm stand or while getting groceries. One weeknight, we would spread newspapers all over the garage floor and carve out our jack-o'-lanterns. My father painstakingly hollowed out the middle, then helped me carve a spooky face. On occasion, he would howl like a wolf or imitate Dracula's voice to scare me, then he would smile his goofy smile, quite pleased with himself.

There are pictures of me as a very little kid dressed as a witch with a green face and as a clown with a big red nose. After I turned eight, however, I was responsible for my own costume and did my best to transform what was already in my closet into something that would pass for a baby or a hobo, though it was a lousy substitute for one of my mom's creations. Still, I always managed to put something together in time for the church costume parade and trick-or-treating, canvassing the neighborhood on the big night, proudly carrying my empty pillowcase.

One thing I hated about Halloween was the masks. My teenage brother, Matt, relished torturing me (or teasing me, as my mother would say), and the Day of the Dead gave him ample opportunity to scared the daylights out of me. Of course, he—and everyone else—thought it was hysterical to chase me around the house while wearing some terrifying mask. One time, I was so afraid that I hid in my closet for ten minutes, my heart in my throat, while he searched me out. When he finally flung open the door and growled at me in a particularly hideous werewolf mask, I wet my pants.

Maybe that's why, despite my love of Halloween, I was usually pretty happy to move on to Thanksgiving. Even though my brothers complained about the boring sit-down dinner at my grandparents' house, I really liked the tranquil formality of the occasion. After watching the Macy's parade and dressing up in fancy clothes, we would drive twenty minutes to my grandparents' house where I would wish them a happy Thanksgiving and thank them for buying me the dress I was wearing. Then as the adults on my dad's side of the family mingled, I might slip into my grandparents' bedroom to look at the black-and-white high school portraits of my father and his sister, or maybe examine my face in the magnified mirror my grandmother kept on her vanity. Mostly, I would pass the time hiding amidst the cypress trees that surrounded their house or I would bat around the tennis ball hanging from the garage ceiling. My grandpa kept an ice chest filled with orange and grape soda for our visits, which was the highlight of my afternoon.

When it was close to dinnertime, I followed my grandma around the table, placing the forks on the napkins and making sure all the table settings were complete. She put out an ecru tablecloth and beige placemats, as well as two tapered candlesticks in the center of the table, a setting befitting the formal dinner she prepared, complete with turkey, stuffing, mashed potatoes, and a gravy boat in the center of the table. All of it tasted bland, except for the buttery rolls, but I didn't care. All I cared about was, for one day out of the entire year, my whole family sat around the table together.

After Thanksgiving, the Christmas countdown started. The most wonderful time of the year, filled with sweets and presents and carols, seemed to infuse everyone with an extra bit of good cheer. My mom set up a corner of her room as a wrapping station, and she started baking every kind of cookie in anticipation of school bake sales. She let me borrow some of her prettiest earrings to wear for the school concert, while my dad spent weekends decorating the outside of the house in twinkling colored lights and lining our walkway with giant candy canes.

The centerpiece of our holidays was the tree, adorned with shiny, round ornaments and a handful of keepsake treasures collected over the years. My mom was a stickler about our tree. She didn't want it to have any unsightly bare spots, and she debated over which one to choose from the lot while the rest of us looked on, annoyed. Once we got it home, my dad would set it up in the corner of the family room right in front of the window so that everyone could see it as they drove past. I remember sitting by the tree with my parents, watching Chevy Chase proceed to have the worst Christmas vacation ever, laughing and bonding over our shared sense of humor while nibbling on my mom's homemade fudge. In those moments, it was every bit the season of miracles.

On Christmas Eve, we usually went to my grandpa's house where my mom's family gathered every year. As soon as we arrived, the familiar scent of spiced oranges and cigarette smoke filled my nose. A few distant relatives would offer an affectionate hug, ask a few questions about school, and then disappear into conversation and cocktails. Listening to classic Christmas songs muffled by excited chatter, I would find my way into the kitchen in search of the sweet-and-sour meatballs guaranteed to be simmering in a Crock-Pot. I'd fill my plate with all kinds of delicious samplings from the holiday buffet and eat it happily. As the night went on, ice clinked into tumblers and splashed with fancy holiday whiskey, which meant we would not be going home for quite some time. I would then meander into a back bedroom and lie on my back, counting glittery sparkles on the popcorn ceiling until it was time to make the drive home.

When Christmas morning arrived, I would shoot out of my bed to find our stockings brimming with wonderful surprises. Mine was the biggest, and the only one made with beautiful floral fabric. After pouring coffee, we would gather under the tree and open our gifts. My mom's writing, not disguised at all, neatly conveyed the giver and the recipient of each gift—except for a small pile of gifts from us kids. I enthusiastically ripped open the beautiful papers, pulling out dolls and new underwear and hair bows. With the leftover ribbons stuck all over my head, I felt like a princess surrounded by so many wonderful, expensive things. Every little thing about the holidays brought me joy and comfort, just like the holiday songs and movies promised.

These comforts weaved together to form the solace of my childhood years, and I used these fragments, these bits and pieces, to narrate my very own origin story. As a very young child, I was already authoring my own life. I knew I needed to tell a story, the kind of story that ended in "happily ever after," so I picked my moments carefully. I let them roll around in my head, like ice cream melting on my tongue, savoring their deliciousness and purposefully committing them to memory. I wanted to be able to pull them out whenever I needed them, and somehow, I knew I would need them.

I depended on these moments to prove to myself that my family loved me, even when I wasn't so sure. Throughout the years, whenever a thought crossed my mind that perhaps things in my house weren't as they should be, I was quick to satiate any doubt with one of these shining examples of familial bliss. These little moments, nurtured and exaggerated over time, formed the scaffolding necessary to build myself into an adult.

# Three

When I was five, we moved to a suburban community near Los Angeles. Nestled in a green, hilly hideaway, this town where apricot orchards once reigned supreme had attracted a lot of families looking for a bedroom community within commuting distance to the greater LA area. Back then the town was small and familiar, boasting a mom-and-pop grocery, a creamery ice cream shop, and an untouched downtown built along a forgotten train track. My hometown had a quaint, peaceful feel. I played soccer, went to Girl Scout meetings, and learned to play the flute. Everyone joined in the annual summer parade down Main Street, and we proudly watched our very own chorus teacher perform on stage with his band. For many years, everyone seemed to know one another, and we all agreed it was a wonderful place to grow up, even if we didn't have our own movie theater.

However, like me, the town was growing. Track housing spread like wildfire, pushing agriculture to the outskirts of town. Our schools grew alongside us, a new one opening every few years, and retail centers sprouted up all over. Grocery chains, restaurants, and a K-Mart came in, most of which would be replaced and remodeled by the time I got married. Not only was our population expanding, but our ego was too. We shared a collective feeling of both relief and pride when the first McDonald's arrived—our little town was finally on the map. It was as if our community had something to prove, and the constant one-upping became a permanent part of our town's personality.

My family had come from modest means, but through hard work and perseverance, we earned a place in this rat race, living in a nice house on a beautiful street with a lot of kids. My parents were regulars at church, my mom leading the Christmas boutique and selling articles like rosaries and jewelry after church once a month, and they were always at school events like football games and concerts. By the time my brother graduated high school, however, our town's rush toward bigger and better things had evolved into neighborhood shopping. Everyone uprooted to buy newer houses in newer neighborhoods with newer amenities—everyone except my parents. For whatever the reason, they didn't move, and we became entrenched in the outdated part of town. It took only eight years.

Outdated or not, I loved our house, especially the backyard. We no longer had a pool where I could spend hours pretending to be a mermaid, so instead I spent a lot of time on the steep embankment behind the lawn where the avocado and citrus trees sheltered me for long stretches of time. I watched the birds, followed busy lines of ants, and inhaled my favorite smell in the whole world—orange blossoms. It was my favorite place, my own bit of earth and heaven.

## Ordinary Miracles

When I was in elementary school, we were given little redwood saplings in tiny milk cartons to take home on Arbor Day. When I proudly showed my dad, he helped me plant mine in a pot. He oversaw its growth, replanting it in bigger and bigger pots until finally putting it in the ground. For the next fifteen years, he nurtured that little tree into the majestic beauty it is today, planted firmly on my favorite hill. I drive past that old house every now and then, and our tree greets me like an old friend standing eight feet over the cinderblock wall.

I grew up in that small town, in that small house—playing with my Barbie dolls, drawing pictures, taking my dog for walks around the neighborhood, roller skating—happily unaware that there was anything more worth having in the world. It wasn't until I grew into middle school, with its sudden influx of competition and judgment, that I began to notice the current I was swimming in, the constant push for something better, something more.

My mom and dad encouraged us to seek upward mobility and the good life, which was just beyond our reach. Although we didn't want for anything as far as I was concerned, my parents had spent too many years robbing Peter to pay Paul before I was born, and they were tired of hustling. Late hours of overtime, coupon cutting, and generic-brand everything had earned our middle-class stability. When we moved into our suburban haven, they were no longer living paycheck to paycheck, thanks to a posh management position my dad landed in an aerospace plant, but it never felt like we formally "arrived." As soon as we settled into the right house, and bought the right car, a newer model came along and seemed to steel away the joy of what we had. My parents never complained, but the stress of making ends meet had been an unwelcome constant in life, and they wanted us to grow beyond it.

I was just becoming aware of all this when a brand-new high school was erected and I entered as a proud member of the freshman class. A product of my family and my town, I was eager to succeed. Colleges had just begun demanding high GPAs, extracurriculars, and all kinds of impressive tricks to gain admission, so our teenage lives revolved around making sure we had something to set us apart. It wasn't nearly as intense as it would be for students in years to come, but the fervor was in full effect. In a town where we all had something to prove, I got busy proving myself.

A clear-cut path to school had been laid out for me to follow, which was a huge comfort. As long as I followed it precisely, I would find success in terms of grades, honors, and other recognitions. I knew where I stood academically and could gauge my progress—my worth—by letters and numbers sent home to my proud parents twice a year. Proving myself socially wasn't so easy.

It's hard to look back at those years with any kind of clarity. From the outside, I was a smart band geek with popular associations. I didn't shy away from the spotlight, giving a speech at my eighth-grade promotion and becoming the president of the band. It seemed I had lots of confidence and lots of friends, and boys weren't uninterested in me. The view from the inside, however, was a whole different story.

Although I was surrounded by friends, I felt completely alone and misunderstood. Sitting amongst a smattering of girls on the quad during lunch, my skin prickled at what I perceived as their judgment and scrutiny. I lived in constant fear that I would be outed as a fraud and everyone would reject me.

    I always knew I was different, that I was marked in some way. I could feel it. There was no evidence of it, no glimmer of fact or circumstance to orient my suspicion, just a deep, unshakable knowing that I wasn't like everyone else. And it wasn't that I was marked for some great achievement or recognition by my peers. Like a cracked would-be heirloom, I was marked damaged. Unworthy. Shameful. Something was inherently wrong with me, but I dared not admit to this for fear that I would be placed on the discount rack with the other unwanted discards. Instead, I tucked this secret deep inside where no one, including me, could find it, and it festered in my bloodstream, encapsulated in an all-encompassing dread.

    I tried to believe that I was simply an angst-ridden teenager who was, like all my peers, saddled with the difficult task of coming of age. We all felt the pressure of having to conform to someone else's standards. We all felt the desire to fit in and the sting of being left out. The only difference was I felt it all with a great deal of intensity, which made me unappealingly dramatic and tightly wound, according to my family.

    My diary entries from that time read like a sad soap opera, filled with unfulfilled longings and self-condemnation. I was convinced that I was deeply disturbed—unlovable, unwanted, damaged. No wonder I seemed dramatic. Without some tangible, external reason to justify my feelings, I was just whining. I didn't want to be a whiner, so instead I berated myself for being so weak and pathetic, promising that I would work harder to make myself into a better person.

I was undeniably anxious back then, although I never really understood that word or how it applied to me. I flitted about in a nervous fervor, determined to accomplish anything and everything perfectly. I fretted about studying, tests, friends, boys, my family, and on and on. Having lived with it my whole life, I thought everyone walked around with a lead bowling ball in their stomachs, threatening to churn their intestines into gurgling lava pits. I also truly feared that failure wasn't an option, and not in the motivational sense. Failure threatened to wipe out my very existence.

Looking back, I had plenty of reasons to be emotional. In a short period of time, our family had suffered a great deal of loss. My mother's best friend, both my grandmothers, and my favorite uncle passed away from cancer, and my great aunt passed away of a stroke. For several years, we had a constant supply of grief and loss. On top of that, my dad was laid off from his aerospace job, and the hospital where my mom worked shut down, making everything feel incredibly unstable—a situation made even worse when my oldest brother had to close his business and declare bankruptcy, almost losing everything, including his wife. All of these events would have been enough to make me feel a bit emotional, especially if I had been permitted to feel something about any of it.

Still, my feelings seemed more exaggerated, and more intense, than my circumstances warranted and that scared me. For his whole life, my dad fought with undiagnosed depression, which everyone passed off as shyness as he was a man of few words and very introverted. My mom would often speak for him, telling me what he said to her in private about how he really felt. I knew my dad mostly through my mom's translations. She never said he was depressed, but I knew it. I could sense it, as if he had a force field of sorrow around him. It was so heavy that I grew up fearing he would kill himself, so I made it my responsibility to lift his spirits.

Seeing my dad like this made me suspicious of sorrow. I didn't like it. I was afraid sadness would engulf me the way it did my dad, and sometimes it did. Whenever it threatened to take me over, locking me in my room with only Jewel and the Counting Crows to keep me company, I forced myself to think of how lucky I was, running through the thousands of horrific things happening in the world that were not happening to me. I forced myself to be glad, even when I wasn't.

As a kid, my mom made me read *Pollyanna*, and it stuck. I've played her "glad game" a lot, the one where you get through difficult times by focusing on things you are glad about, which felt very natural to me. Happy, positive feelings were all I wanted to feel, and there were so many positive things happening when I was in high school that it was easy to ignore the signs that something was wrong.

When the more undesirable feelings came up, I dismissed them as unwarranted, refusing to acknowledge them most of the time. If I was forced to face them, I would purposely turn my attention elsewhere. It was easy to distract myself since I was swamped with schoolwork and activities, and I was eager to admonish myself for feeling sorry for myself. After all, what did I have to complain about? I had a great family, a great life, and all the opportunities I could want. With nothing on which to blame them, I was convinced my bad feelings were either faults that had to be eradicated or, as my mom suggested, a natural byproduct of hormones and exhaustion that could be waited out.

Much like my mind, my body was always something to be conquered—an insolent child who would not behave. I ruthlessly chastised my clavicle for not protruding out the way Kate Moss's did in the Calvin Klein ads. I forced my bladder to wait until it was convenient to search out a bathroom or reluctantly submit to its demands once my abdomen started cramping with sympathy. In my mind, my size 7 jeans were some kind of punishment for being weak-minded and pathetic. I hated my body and mercilessly berated it. It's no wonder I didn't listen to its whispers. Yet faithful and steadfast, it kept signaling me.

I began having horrible dreams, nightmares of being trapped and tormented while others looked on unmoved. I would dream of defiantly running away from my home in a rare burst of anger, a handkerchief tied to the end of a stick thrust over my shoulder, only to turn around and see the entire house consumed in flames with everyone I loved locked inside. These dreams roused my consciousness, but my body remained paralyzed. Trapped inside my head, trying to assure myself that the dreams were not real, I struggled to wake up, instructing my fingers to wiggle, my eyelids to open, anything to break the spell. Eventually, I would jerk awake, soaked in sweat, my heart beating wildly.

Then my hands began to tremble, shaking with tremors as if I had consumed two red-eyes from Starbucks washed down with a Red Bull. I could usually slide them between my thighs and my desk seat or shove them into my pockets so that no one would notice, but occasionally they attracted a worrisome glance. If anyone ever said anything, I just shrugged it off and told them I was stressed.

In the midst of the shakes, I was periodically fainting. My body would surge with a rush of adrenaline, leaving me feeling loopy with my heart racing. Lightheaded and dizzy, my feet suddenly insecure beneath my weight, I occasionally keeled over and smashed my head against a chair or a music stand or a countertop. As a young girl, I found it more embarrassing than anything else. I had already walked out of my body, so I had no compassion for what it was feeling. I just wanted it to stop creating drama.

I kept moving forward with my life, my body a reluctant companion, and adjusted to the discomfort of being me. I knew I wasn't quite normal, which made me try all the harder to act the part of a normal teenage girl. I focused on being my best self, banishing these undesirable aspects of my personality, and it helped. I enjoyed life (for the most part) by focusing on what I was glad about. Every time my body signaled me or my emotions swelled up, I pushed them down and focused on the future—the magical time when everything would make sense and I would once and for all conquer my wickedly insubordinate self.

I had no idea that my body, my longest and truest friend, would be the force to guide me toward understanding myself years down the road. I never appreciated, back then, that my body was my strongest ally. I certainly never imagined that it would be the key to unlocking the secrets of me, finally giving me the chance to integrate all my many colors into the kaleidoscope of a person I am now. I simply lamented the frustrations it brought to my life.

Music was my respite during the toughest times. It was the only thing that calmed me down. Sequestered in my room, I let the familiar voices of my favorite artists soothe me, lyrics and melodies wrapping around me like the arms of a best friend, constant and true. These strangers with their guitars and pianos knew my innermost heart, reminding me that I was not as alone as I feared. Somewhere in the universe were kindred spirits who ached and longed as much as I did. Somewhere out there, people understood.

Early into my freshman year, I decided I needed a boyfriend. It was probably an idea sparked by my mom, who frequently assumed my lack of male companionship was the source of my sorrow. Wherever it started, I somehow convinced myself that a cute boy would make me happy and I attached myself to movie stars like Johnny Depp, fantasizing about being whisked away into a real-life romantic comedy. I pined after the boys in my classes with a burning desire to attract their attention, silently brooding when they didn't turn my way. Then when they did notice me, I confused them by running away as fast as my legs could take me.

One particularly sweet boy, Sean, drove me to look at Christmas lights in his convertible Chrysler LeBaron. As we walked along the streets of a suburban neighborhood, which could have served as the backdrop of any Hallmark Christmas movie, I basked in the scent of his Drakkar Noir and laughed at every one of his jokes. Then I felt the warmth of his shoulder pressing against me and his clumsy fingers searching for mine, the unexpected intimacy of our hands pressing together sending a rush of excitement into my blushing cheeks. For one glorious moment as we meandered along, I swooned as my teenage dream came true.

Then the warmth—that wonderful sensation of passion in its infant stage—suddenly surged into an uncomfortable heat that singed my skin with scornful disgust. To make matters worse, it was accompanied by a cacophony of voices inside my head screaming hateful insults. Overwhelmed by the whiplash of my own reactions, I withdrew my hand. I think I stammered on about being good friends, words falling out of my mouth unattended by thought, as I watched the innocent flame of our young, budding romance burn up in a matter of minutes.

Unfortunately, Sean wasn't the only boy to suffer from my spastic catch-and-release tendency. I lured in a number of eligible boyfriends with earnestly devoted intentions, only to run away as soon as things turned physical. I couldn't understand why my body constantly undermined my mind's efforts to get close to a boy—especially when I was convinced it was the answer to all my prayers. By the time I was seventeen, I had thwarted every opportunity that came my way and considered myself doomed to a lonely existence.

Then something magical happened. I met Kyle. He was tall and fair, and his million-dollar smile lit up the room. I noticed him right away, feeling his presence from across the room at our youth group meeting. All I wanted was to orbit him, but being shy, self-conscious, and a bit too proud, I stayed at a distance. When the meeting ended, however, he walked me to my car, and I found myself talking to him like we'd known each other forever. After everyone had long gone, he was still leaning on the side of my car looking like everything I ever wanted.

By the time I drove home, I was head over heels in love with him. It took a whole day for him to call me, almost twenty-four hours of pure torture as I wondered if he had changed his mind or lost my number. When I heard his gravelly voice on the phone, I could barely contain my giddiness. I don't remember where we went or what we did on our first date, except that he opened the door to his Volkswagen Bus for me and told me I looked pretty.

After our third official date, he walked me to my front door to say good-night. None too eager to part, we sat on a bench on our front porch, and he reached for my hand and held it in both of his as we talked. To my surprise, I didn't immediately recoil. His long fingers, strong and golden from the sun, felt more like home than anything I had ever experienced. When he slowly leaned over to kiss me, I retreated shyly, but his magnetic force was too much for me to resist, so I surrendered. I felt that kiss all the way to my toes, thinking, *This was worth the wait.*

True to my self-sabotaging ways, however, my instinct to run kicked in shortly after that magical first kiss. Thankfully, Kyle was a year older, outgoing, and bold enough to chase me when that instinct kicked in. The first time I broke up with him, I moped around for two days before I answered the door to find a trail of red rose petals leading down the street and around the corner where he stood waiting, flowers in hand. Another time, when I called it quits after some silly argument, he wrapped up a hopelessly romantic mix tape and left it on my car's windshield. I cried through every song.

I was never as free as I was when I sat in his passenger seat, singing along to the radio as we drove through the night with the windows down. Kyle was the first person who saw me for who I really was, not the person I was trying to be for everyone else. With him, I was safe to let down my guard, and I relished the thrill of doing so. In his eyes, I caught a glimpse of my truest self and dared to show it to another ... and he loved me just the way I was.

I spent my teenage years proving myself, not only to my teachers and college admissions officers, but also to myself. At the heart of it all, I was determined to show everyone that I could *be* somebody, and I was terrified I'd fail. With Kyle, though, none of that mattered. I could just exist and that was enough. I already was somebody to him. He was my true north.

During those four years of high school, I gained independence and reached beyond my family's influence to take in the world around me, which was in its own state of flux. My eyes opened to new understandings and new ways of seeing as we approached the new millennium and all its possibilities. I reconsidered the once irrefutable truths of childhood, but only a little at a time, and prepared for a future I could not yet imagine—a future that would take me far away from my home, my family, and my original self.

In a few short years, my world—and my mind—would begin to fracture. I was so focused on where I was going that I didn't recognize that the end of my teenage years would mark a pivotal moment in time, the closing of a chapter I thought would never end and the beginning of something I couldn't yet fathom. Ignorant of what lay ahead, I skipped along happily toward the point of no return.

# Four

My childhood, at least how I saw it, was pretty ordinary. My dad worked a lot and my mom took care of the house, at least until I was in elementary school when she went back to school to become a nurse. I went to school and joined after-school activities. My brother Matt and I fought a lot and I looked forward to weekend gatherings with my oldest brother Derek and his wife, Lori. On the weeknights, my parents and I used to sit on the couch together, watching the TGIF lineup of *Full House* and *Family Matters*, my dad and I occasionally chuckling while my mom watched from behind the pages of a book.

On the weekends, we spent time around the house mostly. My parents were fantastic gardeners, and our yard bloomed with roses, daisies, and all kinds of other gorgeous flowers I would pluck to give to teachers and friends. In the spring, I got to pick the boysenberries growing along our fence, which my mom used to make the best homemade jam. Biting into a slice of warm French bread smothered in those berries was worth the effort every time, even if their nasty thorns did scratch up my hands.

Nothing seemed out of the ordinary about my everyday life. If anything was unusual or out of place, it was me. Between my body's antics, my swings between anxiety and depression, and the inexplicable void I felt inside, I was a misfit in what appeared to be a pretty typical family. All I wanted was to fit in. I yearned to belong to them, but for some reason, I never truly felt like I did.

Following my mother around the kitchen, asking to help with anything and everything, I felt like I was chasing the wind. She was always flitting about in a nervous whirlwind, and she often found it easier to do something herself than to take the time to teach me anything. We spent time together talking for hours, but instead of filling me up inside, our talks always left me hungry for more of her. I was grateful for our talks because my dad, gentle and silent, hardly talked to me. Even when I begged him to, he didn't have much to say. We co-existed like two islands in the same ocean.

I assumed my parents inhabited the adult world beyond my reach, which I thought I was too young to understand. With my brothers being seven and fourteen years older, they were light-years beyond my grasp as well. Given the age difference, I assumed it was my lack of maturity that disqualified me from the inner circle of closeness I thought my parents and brothers shared.

*You'll understand when you're older.* I heard that a lot, along with, *Just wait until life happens to you,* an ominous warning that my youthful opinions—be they liberal inclinations or haughty admonishments—would change once I gained the wisdom of experience. Until then, I was just a little kid who didn't know anything, at least not anything that mattered. Plus, life would inevitably knock me down a peg or two, and from that lower vantage point, I would rue the day I spoke any words that would taste sour when I had to eat them.

My parents believed that education was the answer to everything, which meant I believed it too. I threw myself into school, hoping to make my parents proud with gold stars and perfect attendance. School opened up a world of thoughts I had never entertained, and I became emboldened with knowledge and ideas. I absorbed the reigning philosophy of the 1980s and 1990s that I could be anything I wanted when I grew up. I believed adults when they told me that I had the power to change the world and that drugs would destroy my brain. As a result, I had strong notions about how things should be handled—not only in my family, but in the world—and I couldn't keep them to myself.

In fifth grade, the anti-drug DARE campaign toured our school opining about the dangers of doing drugs, a message I absorbed like a sponge. Not only did I win an award for an impassioned essay on the subject, but I also became the program's missionary in my household. Seized by the freshly fortified terror of losing people I loved, I made it my mission to force my dad to quit cigarettes. Every time he lit up a Marlborough Light, all I could see were his blackened lungs gasping for what could be his last breath. If smoking could kill him, it seemed to me that someone ought to step in and prevent that from happening. I figured that someone was me.

If I saw a pack of cigarettes lying around, I stole them, even if they were on his dresser, in his jacket pocket, or tucked away in a drawer. I considered it my duty to remove them. To my child's mind, my dad couldn't be tempted by something that wasn't there, so I broke them into pieces, or saturated them in water, or stashed them in various nooks around the house. For weeks, my dad stormed about in a cloud of agitation. *Knock it off! This is not a game!*

I never relented, and eventually, after more than twenty years of smoking, he stopped cold turkey. No patches, no gum, not even an obsession with sunflower seeds. I'm not sure what convinced him to quit. It might have been the obvious cost to his wallet or the risk it posed to his health, but I've always preferred to think it was my love for him that did the trick. I felt immense pride thinking that my antics had some small role in making sure that my dad wouldn't die of lung cancer. (Years later, my dad battled tongue cancer, and I thought back to breaking those cigarettes, wishing I had done it earlier.)

As I got older, I stood up more and more often for my beliefs. At school, my efforts were rewarded with good grades, but at home my passion and zeal were seen as a nuisance. For two years, to protest the inhumane treatment of animals, I ate burgers without the juicy patties my dad seasoned and grilled to perfection. I raged against sexism and double standards at every opportunity. I initiated political discussions without an appreciation for the polarizing sensitivities they triggered. Even if I had realized that I was irritating—poking and prodding at emotional underbellies—I don't think I could have stopped. Being outspoken felt powerful, and it was better than being invisible.

I was finally able to engage with my family on an intellectual level, which was everything. When my brothers debated me, picking apart my every word, their whole bodies scoffing at my brazen stupidity, I felt accepted. When I was able to stand on my own two feet, despite their constant attack of my viewpoint, I felt I had earned their respect. I believed I had finally argued my way into a seat at the table, which in my mind meant I was on my way to truly belonging in my family.

In finding my voice, my confidence grew. I became emboldened and tackled any topic of discussion, including the murky arena of family conflict, assuming my quick wit and persistence could break through the force field erected around the inner sanctum of my family. Once inside, secrets would be revealed, and the murky fog of confusion would finally lift. Little did I know that this delusion, steeped in my teenage brain, would stubbornly persist long after it had been proven insane.

My family's way of dealing with conflict was a lot like the magic trick of hiding a coin underneath one of three cups and then moving them around in circles until the person trying to keep track of it gets too dizzy to focus. Or maybe it was like a game of monkey in the middle—where I was always the monkey. Either way, I continued to try to track down facts or demand accountability, only to collapse in defeat under the weight of their unending avoidance.

When I was quite young and my parents got into a fight, their voices boomed and doors slammed. I took that as my cue to rush in for negotiations. Since my mom used me as her sounding board, I knew all her resentments against my father and was prepared to step in when they argued and share all the things she wanted to say but never did. I would find my dad, his face hardened and his mind elsewhere, and I'd explain that Mom didn't mean the awful things she said, that she only said them because she was hurt. Then I'd articulate the real reason she was upset, nudging his arm to get him to grunt out an "okay" to relay his side of the story. Then I would run back to my mom and share his side of things, hoping to bring them closer together.

I thought it was all a misunderstanding, and given how poorly they seemed to communicate their feelings to one another, I believed I could clear it up. After all, if an eight-year-old could tell that "it's fine" meant it was really not fine, they weren't fooling anyone. This circular negotiation process went on for years, and over time, I became more and more disgruntled with my role. I couldn't understand why they never made any progress and why they seemed to have the same fight over and over again. I grew angry with their apparent refusal to learn how to work things out in a way that made everyone feel better, finally refusing to interfere unless it got too heated.

My family was objectively wonderful, but I felt awful all the time, a dichotomy that was impossible to understand as a kid. I was too young to know that parents can have flaws, or that problems don't always present themselves on the surface. Sometimes they fester just beneath. This left me confused, constantly searching for answers that would make sense of the emptiness I felt. The only conclusion I could draw was that something was wrong with me.

Growing more and more convinced that my unsettled feelings were due to the fact that I had issues, I settled into minding my own business for a while. It was uncomfortable denying my urge to get involved when our house turned upside down, but I learned to hold myself back. Or at least I thought I learned. It all went out the window when my brother Matt met his wife, Cheryl.

# Five

One February afternoon when I was a fourteen, a girl showed up unannounced at our house. I was home alone and unprepared to answer when she asked to come inside. When she said she went to college with my brother and had come to decorate his bedroom for Valentine's Day, I smiled dumbly and let her in. For the next half hour, I watched as she taped up red and pink streamers around his bed, filled up a dish with heart-shaped candies, and scattered balloons all around. She didn't volunteer much about herself, and since I was too nervous to ask, I watched her in relative silence until, satisfied with her handiwork, she packed up her plastic shopping bags and left.

The next time I saw her, she was formally introduced as my brother's girlfriend, the expectant mother of my soon-to-be nephew, and the newest inhabitant of the bedroom right next to mine. The sudden appearance of this woman in my life—and in my house—was unnerving. I knew nothing about her, except that she had an affinity for circus peanuts. She seemed nice enough, with her cheeky smile and blue eyes, and she went to the trouble of making a romantic gesture for my brother, which was sweet. We weren't even that far apart in age, although the leap from high school to college was a big one. Still, I was quietly optimistic. I had always longed for a sister, and now I had one.

I tried to befriend my soon-to-be sister-in-law and be supportive, but it was extremely awkward. All of a sudden, we were thrust into an intimate living situation without any preliminary preparations. Cheryl didn't engage in the usual small talk, let alone the deep stuff. She didn't ask any of the get-to-know-you questions; she didn't inquire about our family at all. She wasn't interested in me, practically ignoring my existence. For the first few months, we merely cohabited as housemates.

I would come home to find her scrapbooking supplies sprawled all over the living room, a move I interpreted as a dog's territorial urinating all over my space, forcing me to retreat to my bedroom to do homework. My toothbrush, scrunchies, and deodorant were relegated to the peeling contact paper under the sink while my prized bathroom drawer became home to her smelly perfume and face powder. She sat on my side of the couch, ate my mother's cookies out of the pantry, and left piles of her stuff all over the house. Had we been proper roommates, I suppose we would have held a meeting to make rules and label our belongings, but we were family with none of the benefits.

In the beginning, I assumed that I was overreacting. She was probably just as uncomfortable as I was—more so, I imagined, because she was living with a strange family while growing a brand new one. I may have been young, but I appreciated her predicament.

At night, Matt and Cheryl would fight like cats and dogs while I lay in bed, my stomach in knots, trying to ignore the screaming and cursing. They would fight about all kinds of things, hurling obscenities and below-the-belt remarks like daggers. My name would come up at some point, and I'd hear them calling me names, the insults piercing the thin wall into my room. I tried to ignore their venom, but it was impossible. They fought all the time. Then, to confuse my adolescent brain even more, they made up as passionately as they fought, so it felt like there was never a quiet moment.

Bursting at the seams, I turned to my mom for relief, listing my pent-up teenage grievances and asking her to intervene somehow, but my mom would only hush me and offer one of her many lines: *Don't rock the boat. Let it go. Do it for your brother and the baby. Do it for me.* So every time I felt offended, confused, or otherwise uncomfortable in my own house, I obeyed my parents' dictate to keep it to myself. Let it go. For the sake of the baby.

Before I could drive, a friend drove me to high school in the morning, and either my mom or another friend would bring me home. On rare occasions, Matt and Cheryl pitched in. On one of those days, we had a mix-up about where to meet; I went to the back of the school, and they went to the front. Several minutes later, I went to the front, and they went to the back. It was pretty comedic, but none of us saw it that way. By the time I got to the car, they were put out because they had to wait so long, and I was irritated that they didn't know where to meet.

My brother leaned in right away. "Where the hell were you?"

His tone put me on the defensive, and I started in, explaining my side of things. As I talked, Cheryl snickered in the front seat, making my stomach churn, forming goose bumps on my arms.

She condescendingly tossed her head, flipping her hair over her shoulder like a snotty cheerleader, and told me I was lucky they picked me up at all.

"In fact, if you're going act like that, you'll end up walking home next time. Right, Matt?" She flashed him a wicked smile before sneering at me. "If I were you, I'd be very nice to us."

I sat in a puddle of my own shame for the rest of the ride home, silent and complacent. I couldn't believe that this woman, basically a complete stranger, would treat me this way. I couldn't believe that my family not only allowed it, but tacitly approved of it by telling me to keep quiet and make her happy. I went to my mother, outraged at the constant jabs that came my way. *You need to get a thicker skin.*

I took her advice and tried to deal with their constant jabs and the unending discomfort of coexisting, but my silence translated into meek submissiveness. They had the upper hand and they knew it, evidenced by their arrogant smirks and oh-so-clever slights. *Ha ha ha ha, isn't that funny?* However, there was something savage about my response to all this. As usual, my emotions regarding Matt were guttural and raw, pulsing with electricity unwarranted by the circumstances. When it came to him, it was as if I was guarding a time bomb of primal emotion. For the most part, I managed to stifle my rage, but it would inevitably explode and I would loathe myself for failing to master my wickedness.

Once, my body shaking with outrage, I shouted that I hated him and he could go to hell. My mom's eyes flew open in disbelief, then she sent me to my room. Moments later, she came in and sat on the edge of my bed. With maternal softness, she gently explained that my brother and his wife were adults and could do as they liked, but she had to discipline me because I was still a child. I argued that if I was still a child, she should be protecting me. She shouldn't let grown-ups treat me the way they did. She should step in, maybe have a family meeting or something. She just patted my arm and left.

By the time the holidays came around that year, tensions were high in our family. Months of repressed feelings—on both sides, I imagine—had turned sour and were bubbling up with a nasty stench. Derek and Lori came to stay with us over Christmas. Privy to the insanity that had invaded our house, they joined in a venting session with me and my parents. Everyone chimed in about some hurt feeling or rude remark, agreeing that something had to be said to Matt and Cheryl. I was relieved that everyone was finally addressing the elephant in the room, and ecstatic that it was finally time to fix things.

Nervous anticipation filled the air for days. I waited for someone to start the conversation, but no one did. I figured it was only a matter of time, so I went along with trying to act like everything was fine even though it felt wrong and awkward. As it grew dark and drinks were poured on Christmas Eve, however, I couldn't take it any longer. Ignoring my churning stomach and jittery hands, I decided it was time to speak up. I was the diplomat of the family, after all.

Within minutes, Matt and I were pitted against each other like boxers in a ring, my entire extended family on the outside like spectators. I tried to articulate the problem, but he dissected my thoughts into sentences, then into words, and then letters, and then random markings, until every one of my sentiments fell meaningless to the floor. He demanded evidence and proof, but what I offered was insufficient and somehow a fragment of my imagination.

Meanwhile, Cheryl fumed silently, her anger leaking out in alternating huffs and eye rolls. I eventually addressed her directly, since she clearly had something to say. She theatrically stormed off to the bedroom, stating that she was "far too mad … far too mad …" at me. She and my mom occasionally hollered things from a safe distance, but refused to engage in the conversation.

Hours went by as I was flung from one side of the ring to the other, foolishly emboldened to reach some kind of understanding or, at the very least, prove that I wasn't crazy. No matter how many times Matt verbally knocked me down, I got back up. Over and over again, he deconstructed my perception of reality and made me feel crazy. Without any help from the rest of the audience, I forged ahead in a desperate attempt to be heard. I unearthed concrete examples and offered potential solutions. I switched from saying, "you this," to "I feel that." I was becoming nimble in my arguments and hopeful that we could reach a compromise of some kind. Then, just as I thought I was finally getting my point across, Matt switched tactics.

"What does evil mean to you?"

"Huh?"

"Evil. What does it mean?"

I stammered, trying to come up with a definition while wondering what this had to do with our predicament. After attempting to define it, my brother looked at me with scorn.

"How do you think it feels to be called "evil?"

My stomach dropped.

"You called me evil," he said somberly, shaking his head.

"I didn't call you evil."

"Yes, you did."

I couldn't remember calling him evil, although given our spats, I couldn't be sure I didn't. I started to doubt myself.

"If I did, I probably said it because I was angry and didn't really think through the whole meaning of it. I wasn't trying to say you were Satan's spawn."

"How do you think that felt?" he persisted.

"I'm sorry," I said, trying to swallow my anger. "I shouldn't have said that."

"You have a sharp tongue and you can really hurt people."

"I'm sorry."

Matt went on and on and on about how hurt he was that I used that word in reference to him. As he circled around this harm, my list of complaints went out the window. Nothing I said compared to me hurling the word "evil" at him as if it were a weapon. All my opinions were null and void. All my hurt feelings were inconsequential. And I didn't remember ever saying it in the first place.

When I finally had enough and tried to end the conversation, I was lambasted for running away like a little kid and prodded to defend myself. I was forced to participate fully because as Matt not so subtly pointed out, I was the one who started it. I was the one who had a problem, not them. So I had to sit there and finish it. The only way out was to admit defeat and apologize for being wrong about everything, which I ultimately did.

Looking back, I can see that I had been sent out like the

henchman to take care of the dirty business of telling the truth. I wasn't permitted to speak openly or resolve things in a normal manner, but when the time was right, they wound me up like a toy soldier and sent me into action. I was fifteen.

    I went willingly into this role, thinking that I was going to bring our family together and help clear up misunderstandings, but I was the only one who had that intention. I didn't realize that my family was only interested in letting off some steam. They had no intention of addressing actual issues and understanding one another. Ever. The only reason they fought was to release some of the pressure from a situation that had become too explosive. Then, once the emotion was drained a bit, the situation would be put back in its rightful state of denial. Their protocol for conflict resolution was to deny, then vent, then get drunk and shout, and then wake up in a blissful state of denial again. My mom said it was part of being Irish.

    For twenty solid years, I prepared for battle, adjusted my strategies, and did everything I could to have an honest conversation with my family—about anything. I was convinced that I could find a way to use my voice to actually resolve something with at least one of them. It never worked. Still, like an idiot, I kept trying in the hopes that I would win them over and eventually be brought into the fold. I had no idea I was fighting a battle I was destined to lose.

# Six

In trying to make sense of the confusion I felt, I've spent a lot of time piecing together my family's history. I thought if I understood more about my parents and the lives they lived before I came along, maybe my life would make more sense, that if I could make sense of it all, I would feel better. That's what I wanted.

Unfortunately, too many details have been purposely left out of stories, some have never been told, and others turn out to be fabrications when tested against public records. To this day, Aunt Karen is still unsure whether my great-grandmother died while giving birth to my grandpa's youngest brother ... or if she faked her death and lived out her life well into her eighties in a nearby town. I suppose I'll never know the full story of the people from whom I've descended, but the fragments I do know shine a light on the world I inherited.

Like many families, the Great Depression left a lasting impact on mine, especially on my father's side. My grandpa Harry was one of four kids born in Missouri to Irish and Finish immigrants. I was told that my grandpa's mother died in childbirth after their youngest was born. At that point, the baby was sent to live with another family, their sister was sent to yet another family, and my grandpa (just barely a teenager) and his oldest brother traveled with their father to Washington where they worked as farm laborers. By the time my grandpa was eighteen, he was apparently tired of picking fruit and joined the Air Force. Very soon thereafter, he started a family with my grandma in California.

My grandma Betty was one of four sisters who found themselves in a similar situation after their father died. One by one, they followed their mother out of their home state of Nebraska to live in California—except for the oldest who got married and stayed behind. My grandma was the youngest, a little girl of only seven years.

I think my grandparents married with the hope of creating the kind of stable family life they missed out on themselves. After moving with the military to Alaska and Newport News, they came back to California and bought a nice house in the San Fernando Valley. They had my father and Aunt Karen, the so-called millionaire's family, and set up the kind of life that included Sunday dinners, a collection of Hummel figurines, and a beautiful rose garden in the front yard. By the time I was born, they were the typical grandparents who came to my band concerts and bought nice presents. To me, they were the real-life version of the Norman Rockwell painting that hung in their living room for years.

My dad grew up in the era of classic cars, drive-ins, and crew cuts—and it suited him. He was a handsome young man, and his unique combination of dark eyebrows and blond hair emphasized his dreamy hazel eyes. He looked like he could have been on the old television show *My Three Sons*. Being shy, he never talked much about his childhood. The most he would share was about vacations at Lake Tahoe and his time in Alaska, which he thought was the most beautiful place in the world.

Without any conflicting information, I was content to believe they were a picture-perfect family. It wasn't until I was in middle school that I started to realize that my perception of them was more fantasy than reality. Around that time, I began to hear things.

It started with my godmother, Great-Aunt Pamela, a very classy dame who was once married to a wealthy man, and they lived in Beverly Hills. I always thought of her as a glamorous movie star from a bygone era in her pencil skirts and cardigans with broaches, heels, and lipstick. When I hugged her, she smelled like the perfume counter at Macy's. I remember getting a check from her on special occasions, wrapped in a crisp, white envelope, tied with a fancy ribbon, and addressed in perfect cursive.

When she passed, however, I learned that she had an estranged adopted daughter, whose childhood was not so fabulous due to my great-aunt's alcoholism. As a young girl, her daughter went to live with relatives to escape the tumultuous, neglectful situation, and their relationship never recovered. They eventually stopped speaking and lost contact altogether. Everyone must have stopped talking about this long-lost daughter because I never even knew she existed.

After Great-Aunt Pamela died, however, her daughter flew in from out of state for the funeral. She wanted to pay her respects, which turned out to be the wrong terminology for their situation. In order to gain some kind of closure, I think what she did was say her good-byes, which were not as affectionate as they were healing, because my family salvaged boxes and boxes of Great-Aunt Pamela's belongings from a dumpster where her daughter had thrown them. She was obviously still angry at the woman responsible for her upbringing. We unpacked unopened boxes of heirlooms, china, jewelry, and old photos collected over a lifetime, a lifetime from which her daughter did not want a single keepsake.

While this news was shocking, I was even more surprised to learn that Grandma Betty was also an alcoholic. She was a quiet drinker, hiding a can of Coors under the cabinet or slipping away to the kitchen to take a sip or four, so I never knew about it. She never seemed intoxicated to me; at least she never acted the way my parents did when they drank. When she became ill and went into the hospital, she morphed into a cantankerous old woman I didn't recognize, behaving nothing like the grandma I knew and loved. She lashed out at the hospital staff and our family, making scenes and hollering orders like a drill sergeant. I had no idea what to make of her behavior, or how to understand what alcohol had to do with any of it.

Then the untapped fury between my father and his sister surfaced, unearthing years of unresolved feelings in fits of explosive fights. The topic of discussion didn't matter as much as the devious, underhanded scheming they both accused one another of doing. Before I knew it, things were just plain ugly and I couldn't understand why. This undercurrent of disdain persisted for years.

Despite angry fights, power struggles, and a lot of gossip, my dad always said, "I don't have a problem with my sister." That was his line. Aunt Karen's response was the same, that she was completely clueless as to where things went wrong. Obviously, something happened to cause such distrust and discord. Maybe it wasn't one big thing, but a lifetime of little things that added up. I'll never know.

That time period opened my eyes to an entirely different side of Grandma Betty, a side that was never confirmed until decades later when I had a poignant conversation with Aunt Karen. She told me that my grandma fell into a deep depression during her time in Alaska, leaving my her and my dad to fend for themselves while Grandma Betty locked herself in the bedroom for days. She also said Grandma often riled herself up into a rage without warning, forcing them to walk on tiptoes around her, and she was known for her silent treatments that lasted for days, sometimes even weeks. It was easier for my dad, Aunt Karen said, because he was Grandma's favorite and could do no wrong. For reasons no one knows, he had a harder time with my grandpa Harry.

At no point did my father mention any of these unsavory details. When Grandma Betty fell ill, the stories came out of the woodwork. But these stories, like the stories that came later after a great deal of pestering, escaped accidentally. My father's side of the family was clearly determined to keep up appearances and never speak of events that would tarnish the family's reputation. My grandma's illness cracked open those closed doors, and for just a moment, the inner workings of their family showed themselves.

Of course, as soon as the grief and upset subsided, everyone resumed their posts and order was restored. Any bit of truth that contradicted the family's perfect image was nullified through lack of attention and, if necessary, outright denial. Tight-lipped and stone-faced, everyone returned to deafening silence when it came to emotional matters. My father's family heard no evil and saw no evil. End of story.

    Unfortunately for me, that is the end of the story as far as they are concerned. Our family tends to bury the truth with its dead. However, the practice of hiding any truth that might sully the family reputation was passed down from generation to generation. As I would soon discover, this inherited trait was already at play in my family of five by the time I was born into it, and it would become so entrenched over the years—so normal—that I would not recognize it for what it was, even when it was right in front of my face.

# Seven

In contrast with my father's side of the family, my mother's history seemed like an open book. Both my grandparents grew up in the Dakotas and fell in love very young. In a snapshot I have of them just after they were married, Grandpa Del looked a bit like Clark Gable from *Gone with The Wind*, and my grandma Iris was a giggling older version of my mom. They were both adventurous and free-spirited, which fueled their decision to set off for California to build their life together.

Grandpa Del drove a milk truck in Los Angeles, delivering to all kinds of celebrities on his route, and my grandma took care of their five children. It was always busy around the house with kids running about, so my mom, being the oldest, looked forward to summers spent in North Dakota with her favorite grandparents. It was hard to get by during those years, but my grandpa still managed to take the kids out for fish and chips on their birthdays, and my grandma made sure the little extra money they had was spent on a stylish dress for a school dance. That's most of what I know about those years because they divorced when my mom was a teenager. Growing up, I only knew Grandpa Del as being married to his new wife, Elsa, and her three kids. Those were the relatives we visited on holidays.

Just as it was with my dad's side, my perception of my mom's family was steeped in youthful romanticism. While I heard things growing up (like how my uncle Robby, Elsa's youngest son, was a bit slow because he did too many drugs), such stories didn't make a lot of sense at the time. As I got older and began more critically assessing who my family really was, I began to appreciate their significance, and I saw those well-known facts come together to form an entirely different story from the one I assembled as a child.

My mom has always been close to her sister, Auntie May. Although they fell out a lot through the years, they managed to come back together time and time again. When she was only fourteen, Aunt May had a son and then, many years later, a daughter from a second marriage, which is when I remember her being a regular part of my life. I loved spending time with her and my uncle Bruce because they were so much fun. He was the life of the party and always made me feel special, dancing with my feet on his shoes, so I was shocked when they divorced. Like everyone else, he drank too much, but it turned out that he also did drugs and beat my aunt up pretty regularly. Years later he died of an overdose while living on the streets. Although she had a few long-term boyfriends, Aunt May never remarried.

Then there was my favorite relative, Uncle John, who was always jubilant and lively. He was married to Marie and had an adorable beagle named Taco. The only years I remember knowing him were the years he was sick with leukemia. My mom said it was such a shame that his life had been so tough—like when he had to stay home from school for a year because his legs were in braces, and my mom threw tea parties for him after school to cheer him up. He ended up dropping out of school and never learned to read, but he managed to get by in life with his abundant charm.

My mom looked out for him his whole life, but she couldn't protect him from cancer. Even after she donated her own bone marrow to save him, he lost his battle when I was in middle school, breaking all our hearts. I made sure "It's so Hard to Say Goodbye to Yesterday" by Boyz II Men played at his funeral, and I still can't listen to that song without thinking of him.

I never knew my uncle Mitch; he passed in a tragic motorcycle accident when he was only eighteen, several years before I was born. His passing hit my uncle George, the baby of their family, particularly hard, as they had apparently been thick as thieves. Uncle George lived in Ohio, then Florida, so I never really saw him as a kid. When I did, he usually came around with his son Tony, the only cousin who was my age. Tony was an adorable sweet-talker, but he was mischievous. He struggled with keeping his life on track and later died of an overdose while serving a short jail sentence, leaving behind a broken family. Uncle George took in Tony's oldest child and raised him for several years, but cancer came for George and took him from our lives as well.

The person I knew the least was my grandma Iris, whom I saw only a handful of times. She wasn't a regular part of my life growing up, and my mom didn't share much about her, though I remember her as very petite and funny. She had a quiet spunk to her that I loved. Her third husband, Jack, was a hilarious sort and loved the spotlight. He also watched a lot of videos, renting seven or eight movies at a time and then binge-watching them before bingeing became a thing. All I really remember about Grandma Iris is that she worked at Burger King near the end of her life, becoming a den mother to the group with whom she worked. She was happy, it seemed.

When I was in eighth grade, my mother learned that Grandma Iris was sick with an advanced-stage cancer. Although she had told my mother about some doctor visits over the phone, Grandma had clearly downplayed the severity of her illness. My mother was furious that Jack had not taken better care of her or told us how severe her illness had become. My mom never cared for him, and she particularly despised the fact that he never called. Mom paid for a plane ticket for the next day and demanded that Jack get Grandma Iris on the plane. He did.

When Grandma Iris arrived, I barely recognized her. She was frail, thin, and riddled with lumps all over her body. It was so shocking to see her that way; I was frightened, but I knew I had to be there for her. My mom moved me out of my room and into the dining room, setting up a cot next to the window where I could sneak a peek at any visitors waiting at our front door. A few of my belongings were stacked next to the cot, and my grandma was set up in my room.

For the next couple months, I spent as much time with my grandma as I could. I became a cheerful pusher of Ensure milkshakes so that she could get some nutrition, and I wrote out all the prayers I knew so that she could read them in bed when I wasn't there to say them for her. She liked having the late-night television shows on in the night, and the applause would wake me. I'd stumble in to check on her and turn the TV off. Sometimes she'd stir, telling me to leave it on. She liked having the company, I guess.

Like most people in my family, she shared very little about her own life with me, but being a kid, I probably didn't ask the right questions. Even if I did ask the right ones, however, I'm pretty sure she would have held her life close to her chest. As a result, her earlier experiences, especially those with my grandpa, have been erased from my history like pages torn out of a book.

As far as I can tell, my grandparents loved one another in the beginning. Whatever happened in the time leading to the arrival of their fifth child, things had clearly changed by then. My mom said my grandpa dropped my grandma off at the hospital before work to deliver their fifth child and picked her back up on the way home. When Mom came into the house, Grandma showed her the baby. As my mom fussed over the cute new addition to the family, my grandma quipped, "I'm glad you like him. He's yours."

I later learned that Grandpa Del had been physically abusive. Occasionally Mom offered a tidbit of insight, but it was dropped just as quickly as it was divulged: My grandpa would come home drunk at three in the morning and yank my grandma out of bed to make him something eat. He dragged my disobedient aunt by her hair for two blocks. He beat my uncles with a rake in the front yard, causing a week's worth of absence from school. Given how little my family shares, I am quite sure these stories are not only true, but merely a sampling. However, my grandpa's temper was nothing compared to what his own father was capable of, according to my mom.

Mom said that Grandma Iris sunk into herself more and

more. She would sit at the kitchen table, painting her nails, then remove the polish and start over again. And then again. For hours. My mom, the caretaker of the family, made sure the house was clean and everyone was fed. She bore the burden of trying to hold her family together. By the time Mom was in high school, my grandma snapped. She left my grandpa and—having no other choice—the kids too. Already primed for the job, Mom was her replacement.

I never knew this side of Grandpa Del. Although he always seemed like a tough old bird, he had mellowed with age and didn't seem capable of that kind of brutality. He babysat his grandchildren, paid Catholic school tuition for his granddaughter, and volunteered at the food bank. Everyone came to him when they needed help, be it a loan or a place to stay, and he never refused. He was a generous, hardworking man in my eyes. Other than the annual jab at my mom's extra five pounds, he was harmless, yet my mother was afraid of him. There were reasons for that, reasons we brushed aside as bygone stories of a different time with no relevance to our everyday lives.

I'm not sure how Grandma Iris ended up in Florida, but her presence there was the reason my Uncle George moved to Florida for a stretch. Despite being close, he never really forgave her for walking out on her kids. He grew up without his mom and became the unfavored stepchild of an unkind woman, which shaped his worldview in more ways than one. He forever idolized my grandpa, in spite of all his shortcomings that came in the form of bruises. He resented my grandma her whole life for leaving.

I've thought a lot about this division of loyalty, which I always thought was because my grandpa stayed, the fear of abandonment being so much more devastating than a few lumps. My grandpa remarried to give his kids a mother, and despite the dysfunction and physicality of that union, he provided for his kids. He gave them a home, a place to go on holidays, and a spot of money when they needed it. He didn't leave them. She did. A child will never think there's a good enough reason to leave, and yet, feeling all that disappointment, he still moved to Florida to live near her for years. I suppose that was his way to finally feel close to the mom who was always beyond his reach.

When Grandma Iris was nearing the end, we kept a constant vigil. Family members came to say good-bye, including Grandpa Del, and they shared a private moment behind closed doors. Later I would learn that he asked her, "We did have some good times, though, didn't we?" She refused to answer him. I'd like to think that was his way of making amends, insufficient as it was, but it was too late for my grandma.

During her last moments, my brother Matt and I held her hand and said prayers with her. As her breathing began to change, I felt her slipping away. It was scary and overwhelming, but I wanted to do the right thing. I wanted her to feel our love as she left this world. Meanwhile, Mom flitted about in the hallway like a nervous chicken. She couldn't be there with her own mother. She just couldn't. There were probably a million reasons why, but she never shared them with me.

Like my dad's family, my mom's side of the family had a lot of history that was forced into the shadows, shoved aside because nobody wanted to live amongst those memories. Nobody wanted to admit that there were a lot of wounds that needed to be healed. It was easier to pretend they weren't there.

# Eight

I've gone through my family's history over and over again, trying to make sense of all the events that have conspired to shape the people who eventually became my mom and dad, but most of my understanding relies heavily on conjecture. There are some hard facts, like deaths and births and relocations, but the emotional landscape surrounding those events remains hazy. It's difficult to know what moments impacted them the most. With one exception.

There's one moment, without a doubt, that shook my parents to the core and sent aftershocks into the next generation. That one moment has shaped my life in countless ways I can't even articulate, even though it happened years before I was born.

My parents met at a drive-in movie during the summer before my mom's senior year of high school. A year older and brand-new to the workforce, my dad was soon spending every paycheck on making my mom happy. By the time Mom graduated, she was brimming with motherhood. They got married at the courthouse, moved in with my dad's parents, and within a few short months, welcomed their firstborn child. My parents grew up alongside my oldest brother, learning how to parent as they went. Diapers were changed, shoes were thrown, and somehow, they managed to save enough money to move out of my grandparents' house. It was a difficult time, but they persevered.

A couple years later, they were settled into a small duplex and the proud parents of a brand-new baby girl. Born two years after my brother, Samantha had auburn hair and my mom's brown eyes. She was beautiful and, according to everyone, she was a very sweet baby. Now that they had one boy and one girl, their family felt complete. Another millionaire's family. Everything was perfect. My parents, content and happy, set their sights on building their future.

Then, one night, the unimaginable happened. The day after her first birthday, Samantha drowned in the bathtub. It was a freak accident that happened so fast, nobody knew how to handle it. There weren't any answers, and even if there were, they were wholly insufficient because they couldn't bring her back. Even though her death was an accident, my parents carried the heavy burden of having failed her. Although they never spoke of it, it was clear that they were crippled by guilt and by the silent resentment they held for each other. My parents' grief over her was deep and lasting, and it festered. From time to time it bubbled up, and when it did, their pain was raw and palpable.

My dad's family didn't talk about these kinds of things, and my mom's family was used to turning to her in times of need, not the other way around. Unsure how to help, the entire extended family encouraged them not to dwell on their loss, but to focus on their little boy. They tried to carry on, but it was especially difficult to do that when my dad's sister Karen gave birth to her first child, a baby girl, just a few months later. It felt like adding insult to their injuries.

I grew up wanting to know more about my sister, but any discussion about her was off-limits. It was too tender, which I understood. As I got older, though, I wanted to know about the child who broke their hearts. I kept her picture in my desk, snuck into the cedar chest to see the red dress my mom sewed for her with the remnants of her prom dress, and read my mom's Dale Rogers book about entertaining angels unaware. That was as close as I could get to their beloved baby girl, and my only sister.

As I got older, her name would surface from time to time. Whenever we lost yet another family member, old wounds reopened, and Samantha's loss became fresh again. Drinks flowed, and tears were shed. During these times a few new details would surface, sometimes confirming, sometimes conflicting with my earlier understandings. When their grief overflowed, they were too weak to keep their defenses up, and a light was shone on Samantha—but only for a moment. In the soberness of the morning, memories of Samantha were banished once again.

From what I learned, her death ushered in a dark period in their lives. In the early years, their grief swallowed them whole. My dad lost his grip; my mom said he would disappear for hours or days. He would jump over the fence of the cemetery at night so that he could visit the gravesite of his baby girl. He became erratic and lost control, causing my mom to reach out to their pediatrician for help. They managed to hold down work and home life, although they both eventually turned to alcohol to numb the pain, diving headfirst into an emotionally charged mission of self-destruction. I'm sure that's an incomplete, somewhat inaccurate summation, but it's all I know.

Somehow, my parents found a way to move on. They had my brother to raise, and after a few years of trying, they were blessed with another baby boy. My dad threw himself into work, and my mom ran the household on a shoestring budget. As far as they were concerned, they were finished growing their family and took steps to prevent any surprise additions to it. The passage of time had distanced them from that awful chapter in their lives, allowing them to hope again.

Then, to everyone's great surprise, they discovered they were pregnant with me. My mom had been doing Weight Watchers and was discouraged because instead of losing the pounds, she was gaining them. By the time she went to the doctor, who insensitively questioned her loyalty to her husband, she was five months along. Once it was established that my mom was, in fact, faithful to my father, the doctor concluded that the vasectomy performed on my father had not been foolproof.

At that point, my parents had two sons, seven and fourteen years old. Having considered themselves past the baby phase, my mother feared my father would be angry. She shared this with her best friend, who sprang into action and delivered a gift of blankets and rompers. Encouraged by her support, my mom broke the news and was surprised to find out my dad was actually happy about having a new baby.

It's hard to think about how they must have felt when I inserted myself into their lives. My parents had just come through the most horrible loss and were finally getting their feet under them. My mom was focused on mothering the older children she had and perhaps contemplating her next moves now that she was almost free from the responsibility of young children. They hadn't wanted another child. Then, against all odds, I was conceived—and, to complicate matters, I was a girl.

Not only was I conceived in direct violation of my parents' executed plans and born of the female persuasion, but I was born a girl with auburn hair and brown eyes, eerily resembling the little girl they lost all those years ago. My mom would sometimes say, her eyes teary, that I was living a life for two little girls. She said the round birthmark on my back was where my angel wings used to attach before I left heaven to come to Earth to be her daughter. In many ways, I was redemption. I was grace. I was their second chance to have a daughter.

Unfortunately, I was also an unwanted reminder of something—and someone—they wanted to forget.

# The Caterpillar

*Although a caterpillar is born extremely small, it eats and eats so that it can grow quickly. As a caterpillar grows and expands, its skin does not stretch or grow. Instead, a caterpillar grows by molting—shedding its outgrown skin—several times as it grows.*

# Nine

It was my mother's idea that I apply to colleges on the East Coast, three thousand miles away. *There's a big world out there, you know.* My mom felt stuck, it seemed. Too many years of staying put, too many missed opportunities had entrenched her into my hometown and stripped away her desire to leave. All the effort to push my brother forward didn't get him far enough. He ended up staying close to home and starting a family he hadn't planned, just like my parents. Now it was my turn, and she didn't want the same thing for me.

Going to college was a big deal for all of us, the culmination of many years of hard work and intention. My mother constantly talked about becoming a woman of substance and my father exposed me to the finer things in life, so I knew where to set my aim. They taught me that my success in school would transfer into success in a profession, and at some point, I would really be somebody—somebody we all could be proud of. They would give me a push in the right direction, but the rest was up to me.

I grew up keenly aware of how lucky I was to have the option of going to college; not everyone was given the privilege.

Furthermore, I was the remarkable second-chance daughter that would do great things in life and bring honor to her hardworking, selfless parents. Melodramatic or not, I felt responsible for living a life for two little girls, and I took that responsibility very seriously. Going to college and making something of myself were integral to fulfilling my obligation. So with the remnants of my mother's youthful aspirations tucked away in my suitcase, I flung myself into the unknown.

While my mother's ambition sparked my departure, my father's steadfast presence ensured it. No matter how many times he drove me to the airport, he always escorted me in and waited for me to disappear down the jetway. I still remember putting one foot in front of the other, my overstuffed duffel bag draped over my shoulder, looking to see if my father was still waiting where I left him.

Each and every time I twisted around, straining my swollen eyes to catch one last glimpse, my father would be there—standing exactly where I left him. My heart would ache at having to leave him behind. It would take all my strength to keep walking forward, resisting the urge to run back to him and forget about college altogether. Once I managed to board the plane and settle into the window seat he insisted on me having, I would look for him again. Without fail, he would be standing there, his hands shoved into his pockets jingling his keys, peering through the glass walls as my plane prepared to take flight.

As a native Southern Californian transplanted to New England, my college years were a lesson in adaptation. I talked faster than everyone else, smiled too much, and lacked the confidence my bubbly personality exuded. Despite all that, I met some wonderful friends who made me feel like I belonged. With them by my side, I joined an a cappella group, made the dance team, and served as a peer counselor—all of which kept me too busy to feel insecure.

It took a lot of strength and courage to live three thousand miles away from home in a strange place. I missed my family, my friends, and most of all Kyle. It was excruciating being apart, but I was convinced that my education on the East Coast was paramount to everything else. My inner feminist, encouraged by my mom's insistence that I become an independent woman, made it impossible to stay in California for a boy. I might as well don an apron and chain myself to the kitchen stove. Still, my heart ached for Kyle.

After my freshman year, Kyle decided to enlist in the Army. I wasn't enthusiastic about the idea, but he was looking for an adventure and a place he could be of service. He was never cut out for a desk job that kept him inside all day. We talked on the phone, wrote old-fashioned love letters, and counted down the days until we would see each other. It was romantic, in a melancholic, pining sort of way. The strain of distance resulted in several break-ups, but we always found ourselves inexplicably drawn back together. I found it impossible to live without him, even from a distance, and he felt the same way. Finally, we stopped fighting our attraction and decided to stick out the rest of our time apart while planning our future together. We assured ourselves that one day it would all be worth it. One day.

During my college years, I grew and expanded in ways I never imagined. I read insightful books, considered global concepts, and conversed in intellectual circles I never knew existed.

I learned from worldly professors from all walks of life, and I traveled from place to place, walking in the historic footsteps of legends I had only read about in books. The world was opening up to me like a flower in the springtime, and I was enchanted with the fullness of it all. And to my great astonishment, I was doing it on my own.

Looking back, I don't really know why my mom encouraged me to go to school so far away. It was a great sacrifice to send me away, not only financially, but because I was such an integral person in my mom's life. I was her biggest fan, her head cheerleader. I made sure she took care of herself, and I listened intently to the goings-on at her work. I made sure I told her I loved her and appreciated her every day, knowing that the men in my family rarely did. Without me, she would be on her own.

I believed, at the time, that she wanted me to go far away so I wouldn't end up falling into one of the many generational pitfalls that prevented our family from getting ahead. She wanted me to have every opportunity to become successful, and she was willing to make the sacrifices to achieve that. After witnessing her selfless caretaking for years, I believed she was taking care of me in the same way. I suspect she also wanted to brag to others that her daughter was away at a fancy private college in New England.

In hindsight, I wonder if she also needed to distance me from my family. I was growing, becoming more daring and headstrong, and that was dangerous. It was getting harder and harder for me to go along, to hold my tongue, to not ask questions. Even Matt knew that if he mistreated me for too long, he would have a fight on his hands. I wonder if my mom viewed my going away for college as a great way to give us space—and hopefully distract me into a far-off future that didn't require a resolution of my past.

I was so busy living this adventure, the adventure I began to honor my parents, that I didn't realize how much I was changing. I was filled with the arrogant boldness of youth, brimming with optimism and conviction. I was trying on new ideas, new philosophies, and proudly quoting the great minds of all time. Admittedly, I was annoying. I didn't see that my roots were being lifted, preparing me for flight while simultaneously weakening the foundation beneath me. Before I knew it, I was graduating and moving on to law school without a clear understanding of who I was becoming—or unbecoming.

After college, I decided to attend law school in Washington, DC. Having spent a semester of college there, I knew I wanted to go back. I was excited about politics and government and all the things that could be accomplished through those channels. Plus, Kyle was assigned to the Honor Guard in Arlington, Virginia, and we were finally going to be living in the same place. Having held onto our long-distance relationship for so long, breaking up and getting back together time and again, we were so happy to be building a life together finally. Everything was coming together beautifully.

The only problem was that in our time apart, we had grown in two different directions. I tried to fit into his world, and he tried to fit into mine, but it was no use. We were no longer moving in the same direction. After one long, painful evening among my law school peers, Kyle made it clear that those people were not his cup of tea. This led to a discussion about our future, wherein I realized I was not built for military life. We fought for a long time, and in the end, we realized we couldn't be together and still be true to ourselves. Two months into our shared life, the one we had been working toward for so long, we broke up.

It was a brutal breakup, full of endless tears and second thoughts. I'd lie awake at night with my guts twisted into knots, wondering how I was going to live without the one person in the world who really knew me. We both understood our lives had already diverged, that we were forging paths in opposite directions, each step ripping us apart at the seams. By the time we said our good-byes, our connection was frayed, but still tangled. He did his part by refusing to contact me for months, which hardened my resolve to stay away from him, and I did mine by throwing myself into my new situation at school.

Weary and exhausted, I dragged myself to class with only my stubborn tenacity to sustain me. I had made my choice after all. I chose a far-away college and a law school education. I chose to keep my career path ahead of everything else, including love, because I needed to be somebody. As usual, I had something to prove. Casualties were inevitable along the way because sacrifices had to be made, but this one ripped my beating heart out of my chest. I wanted it back, but it was too late.

# Ten

In between going to class and cleaning my apartment, I had to find something to keep my mind off Kyle, to ward off the familiar tug of depression. Our law school had a softball team, and while I had no experience whatsoever, I joined because they needed girls. It was surprisingly fun. I ended up going out with that group to bars and hanging out on the weekends. We had a lot of good times together, and it was a great antidote for my broken heart. It also led me, unexpectedly, to my future husband.

I noticed Will right away. Tall and funny, he always seemed to be having a good time. Bigger than life in so many ways, he seemed to know exactly what he was doing at all times. In his button-up shirt and sweater vest, he seemed like an entirely new species of man, and I was instantly attracted to him. He would find me studying in the library and talk for hours about everything and anything. Soon enough, he asked me out on a date.

He arrived at my apartment, smartly dressed in a long black coat, and whisked me away to a restaurant owned by James Carville, a political strategist I had admired since seeing the documentary *War Room*. I was impressed that he not only listened to my nerdy fascination with politics, but he also went to the trouble of incorporating it into our first date. After a lovely dinner, we saw a play at the Kennedy Center. While walking home, he shyly reached for my hand and held it all the way to my apartment.

Two weeks later, I broke up with him. I was still the same girl, running away from boys the second things became intimate. I couldn't help myself. Thankfully, I didn't have to. With a nudge from a few of our friends, Will ran after me and became the second—and last—boy to catch me.

Our love had a life of its own and took off with great speed, though we had both just ended serious relationships and had no interest in going down that road. My heart wasn't fully healed, and I often wondered if it ever would be. Despite swearing that we were not interested in anything serious, we got serious. We got engaged, moved in together, and started planning our life. We were married before we even graduated, something I never saw coming. It's still one of the best decisions I ever made for myself, even though the decision seemed to make itself.

Things changed so fast for me during this time. When I entered law school, my mind was filled with grand notions of social justice and political change. I was excited to change the world with my law degree by working in government or the nonprofit sector. I was going to make a difference in the lives of the poor, the disenfranchised, and the most marginalized, but in that first year and a half, I got distracted—first with my breakup, then with my social life, and finally with my new romance. It happened so quickly, and with such force, that I could barely catch my breath. By the time things slowed down, I had lost my vision.

Many of my peers were vying for the coveted summer positions at private law firms who came to our campus to recruit, selecting only the smartest, most impressive of us. Without a strong vision of what I wanted to do with my life, my compulsive need to succeed led me to throw my hat in the ring. To my delight, I was offered a position. For the summer, I joined a prestigious firm where I worked on corporate litigation and areas of the law I never knew existed, like telecommunications and antitrust.

Suddenly, I was being taken out to expensive restaurants and scoring tickets to concerts and plays. I was flown to the firm's home office for their annual retreat on the lake. I was invited to partners' homes, which were as fancy as they were big. I swooned over expensive pieces of art and fresh flowers displayed in every room, and I relished the catered food and luxurious furniture. My hard work had granted me access to a lifestyle I had only imagined until then.

Having pleased the partners, I was promised an offer of full-time employment after graduation, which was how things worked at that time. It was practically guaranteed, and as I waited for the formal offer letter to arrive in the mail, I basked in my achievement. I was so close to being somebody I could practically taste it. It seemed like my hard work and sacrifice were finally paying off.

Unfortunately, an offer didn't follow. Instead, I was informed that the firm planned to close their DC office in response to a sudden economic downturn. Not only were all of us summer associates out of luck, but a lot of other attorneys were laid off too, including attorneys with families and mortgages and student loan debt. I told myself I was lucky because I still had another year of law school to figure things out, but it was really hard to play the "glad" game.

The loss of this opportunity made me feel worthless. I wouldn't get the paycheck, the swanky office, or the bragging rights. It was as if all my hard work meant nothing, as if all I had learned and experienced was of no value without that external validation of a firm position. Not only had I completely lost sight of the reason I went to law school in the first place, I had lost sight of the person I wanted to be.

The personal aspirations and convictions I had been cultivating since high school—new and fragile as they were—became absolutely irrelevant as I stood outside the locked door to perceived greatness. All the progress I made, learning about myself in college, went out the window. It was my duty to make the most of every opportunity my parents made possible for me, and without this position, I felt like I had failed them and myself. I swore that one day I would find a way to reclaim it.

I'm not sure how, but my life moved on, even without this esteemed position. I was blessed with a clerkship with an amazing judge and thereafter took a government position with some of the best colleagues in the world. It felt wonderful to be an active participant in our government. Although it did have its drawbacks, I felt good about what I was doing.

Will and I planned a beautiful wedding, and we bought our first house not long after tying the knot. We enjoyed being newlyweds and building our life together, side by side. We would meet up for drinks after work, go sailing on the weekends, and embark on whatever adventure called out to us. We also became do-it-yourself experts around the house. In such a short time, an entirely new, unexpected path opened up for me, and it was putting me back on the track I wanted to follow.

The fast-paced evolution of my person that had begun in college kicked into high gear during law school and left me entirely changed. I traveled home as often as I could, each time feeling the distance between me and my family getting bigger. I ignored the dissonance, as did they, but it was clear that the girl I had once been was disappearing. I assured myself that it was probably a phase, a momentary growing pain on the way to adulthood. I couldn't stay a child forever. I needed to grow and expand so that I could take my place as the adult daughter in my family, and when I did, being older and wiser, I'd finally understand everything. Just like they said.

# Eleven

There's something particularly tragic about being born into my family. If I believed in curses, which I might, I would say our lineage has been cursed because just as soon as things begin to go well, something horrible happens to mess it all up. Every generation, fighting to outrun the disappointment and sorrow that plagued their parents, eventually falls into a new brand of despair and dysfunction—that is, if they are lucky enough to avoid being swallowed by alcoholism, addiction, and abuse. Cancer, in particular, seems to be part of the jinx.

My niece was only four years old when she was diagnosed with a serious, rare form of pancreatic cancer, so we circled the wagons immediately to support my brother Matt and his family. She was the only girl in a family of boys, the youngest still months from being born. Cancer had stolen from us so many times before, but to put its mark on one so young was devastating. We struggled to wrap our heads around what was happening and our hearts around her.

My parents, having lost a little girl already, took the news hard. Only months earlier, they had moved across the country to North Carolina as part of a pre-retirement adventure. After several years of economic instability, they were finally the masters of their own destiny, embracing a new chapter in their lives. But with one phone call, they were instantly transported back to a moment they had tried to outrun for most of their adult lives. Years of stifled grief rose up again, crushing my father's spirit, and the freedom and vitality I had seen recently revived in him started disappearing. For her part, my mother went on automatic pilot in an effort to maintain control. All of this seemed like our ordinary response to a family crisis, but it was different somehow. It was too reminiscent of losing Samantha.

The doctors were performing surgery right away to remove part of her spleen and pancreas, so my husband and I canceled our plans to attend my husband's best friend's wedding in Spain so that we could fly to see her and take care of their family. We wanted to be of some use to them in their time of need. My parents and Derek's family did not rush out for several days, leaving us alone to do our best to care for their boys and the house.

Being in our early twenties and childless, we did our best, but it was inadequate. Since I wasn't a mother yet, I didn't realize my efforts were overstepping. When I saw the boys brushing hair out of their eyes, I took them to get haircuts—not knowing that those precious hairs were not to be touched. I tried to clean the house in preparation for my niece's homecoming, acutely aware of her compromised immune system, not realizing it would feel invasive to my sister-in-law. I had the best of intentions, but they paved the road to hell.

One afternoon, I brought the boys to the hospital and went to visit with my niece. Sitting with her and my sister-in-law, we were talking about nothing in particular when suddenly the conversation turned sour. Cheryl was really upset with me and rattled off a list of my offenses. I did my best to talk through it, apologizing for everything, but being contrite did nothing to assuage her anger, nor did my attempts to explain. I grew uncomfortable having this conversation in front of my niece, and went into the hallway.

I walked toward the nurse's station where hospital staff and patients were gathered. My mom was nearby, having arrived the day before, and was sitting on a bench. Within seconds, Cheryl charged out of the hospital room and began assailing me, yelling and screaming, making a huge scene. We were attracting the eyes of onlookers who couldn't understand what the fuss was all about, and my face was turning bright red. I tried to reason with her, but there was no use. She needed to express her rage, and I was the lightning rod.

Eventually, the security guards were summoned. When they arrived, they looked at me like I had done something horrible to this poor, emotional mother. I tried to handle the whole spectacle with as much dignity as I could muster, but it was impossible. Humiliated and ashamed, I stifled my sobs and hid my tremoring hands until I could escape. I couldn't figure out what I did that was so wrong, or how she could still be so incapable of resolving things in a more respectful way, especially given the circumstances. Worse than that, I felt like I was fifteen all over again, listening to her tear me apart through the thin wall between our bedrooms.

I finally bolted from the hospital, quivering and shaking. My body was responding to this event as if my life was at risk. I was used to my body's antics by then, but this one surged beyond what I had grown accustomed to experiencing. My skin tingled with numbing electricity, my heart beat out of my chest, and I felt cold chills running down my sweaty spine.

I saw my brother in the parking lot just before I drove away. I relayed what had just happened, unable to hide how much it affected me. Tired and worn out, Matt shrugged his shoulders. Although I was angry at his indifference, I reminded myself that what they were going through was unimaginable and it wasn't reasonable that worried parents might lash out on those they loved. It was understandable, I guess, but it hurt. And I couldn't understand how, in practically every stressful situation, I was the one taking the brunt of the lashings.

Cheryl dumped her anger on me in an attempt to relieve her own suffering, and I was supposed to silently absorb her wrath, a role I had been expected to play my whole life, no matter who was upset. I knew the way my family viewed moments like this: Cheryl was the hysterical mother who deserved to strike out, and I needed to be the bigger person by allowing her to take her emotions out on me. I was the family's whipping boy. But it was okay because you only hurt the ones you love.

After I left the hospital that day, I told my husband what happened. As I did, I recalled what Cheryl said as she screamed at me. Not only was she upset about me getting her sons' hair cut and cleaning the rugs, but she was mad I was talking behind her back. I paused for a second, trying to figure out why she would say that. I hadn't talked to anyone about her or her family. In fact, I had gone off grid, sucked into their crisis vacuum. I had been doing nothing but taking care of their kids and bringing clean clothes and food to the hospital. The only people I talked to were my mom and my older brother, Derek.

I suddenly realized that whatever I said to them in confidence had been repeated to my sister-in-law. Things I said out of concern were twisted and then used against me. And why? For what purpose? And at a time like this? I couldn't understand it, and I was hurt. Not only had I been served up as the designated punching bag, but they had riled her up before I even got there.

As usual, there were bigger issues to deal with than my emotions, so I managed to peacefully navigate the rest of our time there before flying back to our life in DC. I knew I should let it go, that it wasn't that big of a deal. I had let go of things far worse. For the sake of my brother, his children, and my mother. Given the severity of the circumstances, I knew it wasn't worth fighting. I had been dancing the same dance with these people my whole life, and the steps never changed.

Except, I had changed. Something snapped in me. I could no longer follow those steps. I couldn't allow myself to be mistreated, screamed at, and bullied in the name of love. I was physically incapable of letting this transgression go without some small token of remorse from them. I knew they expected me to let it go, but it was just impossible.

I made this known to my mother, who passed it along the grapevine as she always did. She said she agreed with me that things got out of hand and my brother needed to reach out. I told her that it wouldn't take much for me to move on, just a small gesture or a subtle acknowledgement and I would get over it. I honestly didn't think I was asking for that much.

# Twelve

My mother said that Matt was a doting brother when I was a baby, always carrying me everywhere and lecturing my mom on how to mother me properly. I liked the idea of him being protective and sweet, and I tried to hold onto the way that memory colored my view of him.

When he was old enough to drive, Matt got a pizza delivery job and enjoyed the newfound joy of making his own money, but instead of spending it all on himself, he always made sure to save enough to buy nice presents for everyone. One year, he got me a gold necklace. Another year, he bought me a book of poetry. He was thoughtful that way, and generous like my dad. He took pride in being able to spoil those he loved.

Unlike Derek, Matt was always willing to run into the fray of death and illness. He wasn't afraid of medical jargon or procedures, and he had no trouble becoming an expert on any given topic. He wasn't easily intimidated and never hesitated to push doctors for answers. He was also able to dress a wound or tend to a dying person without getting too emotional, which made him an essential ally during times of illness and death. Cool and unrattled, he was the rock who steadied us during times of crisis.

By the time he had kids, he fell into the role of being a father easily. Unlike most of the men in my family, he liked being a caretaker. He changed diapers, made dinner, and carried around a Lion King backpack full of snacks and juice boxes. He embraced being a parent, and like my dad, took great joy in making memories with his children. Watching him with his own kids, it was almost possible to believe that he cared for me that way once. Almost.

Although I wanted to see the best in my brother, most of what I remember about our relationship as kids doesn't fall into the category of him being protective or caring. Maybe I came along at a bad time in his life. Being seven years old and the youngest, he may not have wanted to be outshined by a new baby—especially a girl. Or maybe my presence changed the dynamic in my family in such a way that turned him against me. All I know is while he may have started out as a loving brother to me, at some point, Matt decided I wasn't worthy of his love.

Growing up, we shared a few moments of tenderness, but they were very few. Apparently, this was a learned way of interacting. It seemed that Derek took things out on Matt as a kid too. Their age gap was the same as ours, putting Matt at a disadvantage. As the story goes, he put up with Derek picking on him for many years. He was the designated punching bag. Then, when he got the chance, Matt passed that role on to me.

My first memory of Matt is him throwing a hard plastic toy at my face when I was four years old and he was eleven. I was swinging on our metal swing set in the backyard when he hollered, "Think fast!" I reacted too slowly and was rushed to the hospital where I received four stitches on my eyebrow. I've always told that story the way I learned it, filled with humor and a nod to kids being kids. Except my memory of our relationship was never of us just being kids.

I was his outlet, physically and emotionally, for as long as I can remember. My first diary that I kept when I was nine includes an entry that perfectly sums up our relationship from my perspective: "I'm so scared right now. I don't know what to do. I was on the beanbag chair and Matt came over and tried to shove me off of it. I didn't want to move and thought it was unfair, so I fought back by staying put. He got in my face and told me he would make my life a living hell if I didn't stay out of his way. I'm so scared."

Matt used to "tickle" me and prod me, provoking me until I reacted. I would try to hit him, but being seven years younger, I didn't make much of an impact. Instead, he would laugh tauntingly and say, "Easy, killer." He would wrestle me until he was sitting on top of me, making me hit myself with my own hands. I reasoned that this was how all siblings acted, but something wasn't right. I responded to his taunting like a rabid dog, filled with a primal rage that I never felt toward anyone else in my entire life. It was not healthy.

Despite our awful relationship, my mother constantly made him help me with math or piano. He was arrogant, condescending, and had a knack for pointing out my insecurities. He picked on me without actually helping, callously observing my stupidity until I lost my temper.

"Any idiot can understand this," Matt would say.

My teeth would clench.

"Are you really that dumb?"

My cheeks would flush with heat.

"Write down the number 2, then the symbol for multiplication," he'd say in slow motion with exaggerated facial expressions. "It looks like an x. Okay? Am I talking too fast for you? Can you keep up?"

My eyes would roll or I'd erupt with a "Shut up!"

"If you're going to act that way, then I'm not going to help you at all."

Things would inevitably turn physical. I remember clawing at him, digging my fingernails into his skin in an attempt to fight back. My mom would blame me for the scuffle, despite being seven years younger, and tell me to stop letting him push my buttons. *He's just trying to get a rise out of you.* Well, he succeeded every time, and she never changed her tune. Since she was the mastermind behind all parenting in our house, unless she insisted my dad get involved to reinforce her decisions, I eventually learned there was no point in pleading for help. Instead, I sought out tutoring from my teacher at lunchtime and quit piano.

The worst of our fights happened when my mother left me in his care. He would slap me and leave a mark, but it would be gone by the time she came home. Once I hit myself on the cheek over and over again, trying to keep the outline of his handprint visible, but she didn't care. *Don't be so dramatic.* Another time, we were fighting about something, and in a rare moment of cleverness, I locked him out of the house. I'm not sure why I did, but the second I did it, I knew there was no turning back. I was going to die.

He was livid. He began searching for a way into the house, which I knew he would ultimately accomplish, so I ran into the bathroom and locked the door, hoping to stay safe until my mom got home. He discovered me in there and pounded on the door.

"Open. The. Door."

I was scared out of my mind. There was no way I was opening the door. For a moment it got eerily quiet. I sat in the tub with my knees pulled into my chest and waited, my ears perked up in fear. On the other side of the door, I heard clanking and a thudding sound. Then the door jolted sideways. He was removing the hinges from the doorframe and taking the door off. I looked around, realizing there were no windows in the bathroom—no means of escape. I was trapped. And that's all I remember.

Our interactions simmered to a hateful sizzle as we grew up. He delighted in talking down to me in his condescending tone, only interacting with me if it gave him an opportunity to feel superior. For a couple years, I tried to use this to my advantage. I pretended to be clueless and asked for his advice on cars, college, boys ... anything that might soften him toward me. It never really worked, and soon we were back to coexisting. When his wife entered the picture, even that was impossible.

The way I saw it, Matt was permitted to act however he wanted at my expense. He could get away with murder and even if he was caught, he'd still be my mother's favorite. Matt had free reign to take his aggression out on me whenever he wanted. Even a complete stranger had been invited to do the same alongside him, and my mom and dad allowed it. Yet I was expected to act like a perfect angel, no matter what he did to me.

# Thirteen

During the entire time my niece was ill, I felt like I was stuck on a roller coaster going around and around until I was so dizzy and nauseated I couldn't tell where I was. I felt torn between my love for my family and my newfound love for myself, and I wanted to do whatever I could to ease the pain of my niece's illness. I wanted to support them, yet I couldn't pretend like everything was okay when it was so much worse than before.

My demand for an apology had severely fractured our fragile relationship. Everyone banded together against me and waited for <u>me</u> to apologize or, at the very least, come crawling back with my tail between my legs. It was solely on me to grovel at Matt and Cheryl's feet, just as it had always been. But this time, I couldn't do it. As Derek would say, there I was again, *creating a problem where there wasn't one*. Even I didn't understand why I couldn't just get over it and go back to how things were. It was incredibly confusing, and I found myself flailing.

Although I had a great job in DC, was married to the love of my life, and had just bought a house, I was miserable. As always, I needed to make sense of myself, so I tried to find reasons for my unhappiness, other than the obvious rift with my family. I needed the cause of my discontent to be something I could actually do something about. Will and I had been trying to get pregnant—with no luck—so I wondered if maybe I was just eager to start a family. Then I started to rethink whether or not my job really made me happy. Then I questioned whether living in DC could be the problem, and eventually, I circled back to my failure to attain that fancy legal job.

I decided that was it: I was unhappy because I never fulfilled my potential. I never got that prestigious job. That was the problem, I assured myself. I should move someplace new and get that job I wanted so badly, then after a little while, I could focus on getting pregnant. That would make me happy, and most importantly, that was something I could actually do.

I put my plan into place and soon landed a litigation position at an international firm, complete with a beautiful office on the thirteenth floor. From my window, I could see the city sparkling below. I took great pride in wearing my suits and heels, filling my mug with French vanilla coffee from the kitchen, and meeting with remarkable minds around a glossy conference table.

It didn't matter that my heart wasn't in my work or that I had gone drastically off course from what I had set out to do as a lawyer. It didn't matter that I had traded in a pretty great existence for one that didn't suit my personality well. What mattered was that I had finally arrived. I was finally somebody, which meant I could finally be happy.

More than anything, I wanted to share this moment with my parents. Although my niece was still sick and my relationship with my family still strained, I truly believed this pinnacle achievement would help mend things. After all, this was the final destination. This was where we had hoped to arrive, way back when I was struggling to understand fractions and playing the part of elderly witness in mock trial. My parents had made it possible for me to have the best education. Their hard work and support opened the doors for me to achieve all they had ever wanted for me. I was now a high-powered attorney, married to another high-powered attorney, and we lived in a beautiful house with several bedrooms for our future children. It was their accomplishment as much as mine.

I thought seeing me reach this new height would remind them of how much I loved them. They would see that I had jumped through every hoop and passed every test in order to harness what they wanted for me. I figured that I couldn't take away their pain or give them smooth relationships among their children, but I could give them this. I could show them that their investment in me paid off. I had become somebody.

The first chance they had to visit, my husband and I drove them to the towering office building downtown. Planning to check out my new office and then grab lunch at a nearby restaurant, I beamed as I pulled into the empty garage on that Saturday afternoon. As I flashed my key card and watched the metal gate open for me, pride and satisfaction pulsed through my veins.

I parked near the elevator, and we all got out of the car. All of us, except my mom.

"Go ahead without me," she said. "I'm just going to sit here and read my book."

I looked over at my mom, camped out in the backseat under a blanket, her nose already buried in her book. I beckoned her to come, wondering if she just needed to know how important it was for her to come along. Maybe she needed me to flatter her a little, remind her that she was a very important person who needed to be part of this expedition.

"No, I'm fine. You guys go on and enjoy."

I stood speechless, realizing she really wasn't going to get out of the car. My husband good-naturedly encouraged her to come with us, promising a cup of coffee as an incentive.

"No, really. Don't worry about me. Go on."

I stared her down, completely immobilized, as my husband and father eyed me warily. She lowered her eyes to the pages of her romance novel, disappearing into a world far away from me.

"Mom."

"Seriously, go ahead. I'll be fine here," she insisted and shooed us off.

My husband reached for my hand and led me away as I tried to pull myself together. My dad noticed my disappointment and tried to look excited enough for two, an awkwardly sweet gesture, as I let us into the building.

Making the best of it, I showed my father every nook and cranny of the office that wasn't on lockdown. He sat in my chair and took in the view from my desk. Having worked in an office, he was well acquainted with the world I now inhabited, and he fawned over all the obvious perks, making a point to show that he was impressed. He tried extra hard to be enthusiastic enough to make up for my mom's absence, which he knew hurt me. I smiled warmly, pretending it was working.

I couldn't understand why my mom refused to see my office, knowing what it meant to me—to us. I couldn't fathom why, after all the years of struggling to get to this point, she would not want to join in the celebration of our achievement. This whole thing started out as our dream. *There's a big world out there.* Didn't she remember? Didn't she care?

# Fourteen

Matt and Cheryl never reached out, and time ticked by slowly, painfully, as we waited anxiously for every report about my niece's health. I was being punished with an unacknowledged silent treatment for stepping out of line, for daring to want to be treated better.

I appealed to my parents and to Derek to intervene, especially since they had instigated the whole thing and were, in my mind, partially responsible. All I wanted was an apology or an acknowledgement that—despite understandably difficult circumstances—it wasn't okay to treat me that way. I said I would forgive Matt and Cheryl if they would just make one small effort—say things got out of hand, say they might have gone too far, say they were grateful that I had shown up. Anything to let me know they cared about how hurt I was.

Having never once admitted to a wrongdoing or even an unintentional mishap, Matt and Cheryl refused, and the whole family sided with them. I was expected to make nice, as usual. Derek went so far as to make a peace offering on my behalf, telling everyone that I would be at the next holiday and bygones would be bygones. Apparently, the rest of the family was annoyed with the rift I had created and decided to put an end to it without my involvement. If I wouldn't make nice, they would make nice for me. I was irrelevant to the situation, provided my body ended up in a chair to be counted.

Despite my feelings, I felt I had to be there for my brother's family during this awful time. Since my body wouldn't transport itself to the holiday gathering, much to my family's ire, I tried to do everything else I could to be supportive from afar. I sent my niece gifts and flowers periodically, sewed a quilt for her, and checked her blog constantly. Because I never spoke on the phone with Matt and Cheryl very much before my niece got sick, we basically talked the same amount. During those handful of calls, I asked about her health and what I could do from three-thousand miles away. Matt never broached the elephant in the room.

As time went on, my niece's health continued to decline, and almost two years into her illness, it seemed that she was taking a turn for the worse. We made a quick weekend trip to see her, knowing that we would have to keep it short and sweet. In all that time, nothing had been resolved. My niece was the priority, though, so we put our differences aside for her sake and spent our time playing with her and her brothers, mostly avoiding any serious adult conversation. As we sat in the living room during our last hour there, the tension finally broke.

"We're all going to Easter at Mom and Dad's, so you better be there." My brother wasn't asking. "It might be the last time our family will be all together. So you WILL be there."

I took a deep breath. "I'll think about it, but we probably won't be able to make it."

Cheryl's nostrils flared. It was clear that she had been holding her tongue the entire time we were there, slipping into the kitchen or bedroom to avoid us at every chance, and she was ready to blow. My skin went cold as her face twitched with pent-up anger. Her mouth opened and let out a string of words meant to strangle me. Yelling and carrying on like a wounded animal, her anguish poured out in every direction. I don't remember most of what she said, but I remember the sting of her screeching words.

"My daughter is dying!"

She must have repeated it two more times as I sat there, frozen. It felt as if she was screaming, "My daughter is dying… *and you're killing her!*" My niece was in the other room with her brothers, listening to every word. Although it shouldn't have been surprising, I couldn't believe Cheryl was talking this way, angry or not, knowing that my niece was within earshot. Matt shifted from aggressively supporting his wife to calmly trying to neutralize the situation, expertly maneuvering like a trained professional well-versed in playing good cop/bad cop.

My heart thudded in my chest, my eyes lost focus, and electricity pulsed through my veins. I looked over at Will, who looked like a witness to a fatal car crash, and begged him with my eyes to save me. He matter-of-factly told them we had better be going, grabbed me by the arm, and escorted me to the rental car.

My brother followed us to the driveway, his words falling in the space between us. My adrenaline was spiked, stripping me of my more sensible faculties. Crackling with fitful spurts of fear, the engine of my mind whirred with one thought—run.

As Will drove away, my eyes rested uncomfortably on my

brother's figure. He seemed so helpless, fragile even, and I felt twinges of compassion and pity for him, urging me to go back and pick up all those words lying on the ground where I had left them. Yet I knew, deep down, that I had to go. My face pressed against the car window, I felt my soul collapse in exasperated exhaustion, draining out of my flesh until I felt as hollow and haunted as a cavern.

For three years, my niece fought for her life like the warrior princess she was. She went back and forth to the hospital, enduring surgeries, chemotherapy, and all kinds of treatments. She attended school, joined Girl Scouts, and tried to make the most of her life. Her parents, doctors, and nurses did everything in their power to make her healthy again. None of it worked.

Meanwhile, I tried to be the supportive sister and aunt, falling short in all the ways that mattered. I prayed and prayed, hanging onto every hopeful word posted in their online updates. I sent cards and gifts. I visited, offering pieces of my broken heart through the bars I had erected around it. For years, I struggled to find a way to be there for my niece and my family without sacrificing my health and sanity. None of it worked.

In a cruel twist of fate, or perhaps divine serendipity, our family's history played itself out before our eyes. My brother and sister-in-law stepped into the role of grieving parents, devastated by the unfair tragedy of the most horrific loss. My brother and I, like our father and his sister, found ourselves unable to salvage a connection to one another; our dysfunctional dynamic reached a fever pitch, causing irreparable damage. And just like my father's sister, I became pregnant with my first child, a girl, who came into the world a little over a month after my niece passed away.

During that difficult period of time, things irrevocably changed. My family suffered the unthinkable loss of a little girl for the second time, and there could be nothing worse. Her illness and passing justified any bad behavior, no matter how wrong, because no one should have to live through such a devastating blow. Having been forced to suffer such a terrible loss, my parents and my brother were given carte blanche—not that they needed it—to behave however they wanted.

At the same time, I had evolved into an entirely different person than the one they raised. I had been out in the world and experienced other ways of being. I saw things differently from them. I no longer believed that my family's way of dealing—or not dealing—with things was healthy. I had become independent and strong-willed, a trait necessary to survive alone, three thousand miles away. I had seen my goodness reflected back to me in the eyes of others, hinting that I wasn't the inferior whipping boy my family told me I was. I had learned to use my voice to defend myself and my feet to walk away when necessary. I knew there were better ways to love, ways that didn't hurt.

My relationship with my family had shifted, and the strain of my niece's illness magnified those changes. I would never be able to fit back into the mold they created for me, no matter how hard I tried. No matter how high the stakes. And they could never have it any other way.

# Fifteen

When I found out I was pregnant, after wanting to conceive for a couple of years, I was overjoyed at the prospect of having a baby. Unfortunately, I was also consumed with guilt over having a life growing inside me while my niece was losing hers. One thing had nothing to do with the other, but my family made me feel like I had spitefully procreated with the express intention of hurting Matt and Cheryl.

Will and I focused on becoming a family and embraced the journey ahead, reading baby books and shopping for car seats and bouncy chairs. I kept a journal, documenting every single kick and wiggle, and wrote letters to my unborn child. We played music for my belly and made sure I ate really healthy. We even wrote up a lengthy birth plan, which later would go right out the window. We had so much fun preparing for our little one.

Of course, some unforeseen scares came up. We took the normal tests and found out that I was a carrier for cystic fibrosis, but thankfully Will was not. Then we found out that our baby might have trisomy 13, a rare disorder with an absurdly high mortality rate. When we found out, we researched the condition and read horrifying stories that scared us into having an amniocentesis done. All of it was pretty scary, but we made it through those nine months, and at the end of it, our beautiful little girl was born perfectly healthy.

It was difficult being a new mother, as it is for everyone. Having decided at the last hour not to return to work, I found myself adapting to an entirely different way of life as a stay-at-home parent. Gone were the days of rushing off to work, having long lunches out, and stopping for dinner on the way home. As soon as my daughter arrived, I barely had time to shower or grab a bite to eat in between diaper changes and feedings.

But I adored that little bundle of love so much that it didn't matter. She was so very precious. With her stone-blue eyes and blond tufts of hair, she was the most precious thing I had ever seen. I was enamored with her and instantly protective, holding her close and doting on her constantly. Having lost my niece, I was acutely aware of how fleeting our time with her might be.

My new role as full-time mom got easier as time went on. I got into a rhythm and started enjoying my time with her. I loved taking her outside and watching her react to the feel of grass and the way the wind tickled her skin. She was curious about everything, but always content to stay close to me. As she learned to walk, she would lead me around the yard and have me smell each and every flower she passed. I basked in her wonder. Loving her came easy to me.

I worked really hard to be the best mother I could be. I read tons of parenting books, pureed baby food, sang her songs, read her books, and carried her everywhere. I started traditions and sewed dresses for her. I saved every memento in a special box and took an obscene number of pictures. More than anything, I wanted to do right by her.

As she grew into a toddler, I started to realize the strain becoming a family had put on my marriage. My husband and I used to spend so much time together, commuting to and from work and hanging out on the weekends. We used to love taking our dogs on hikes or watching movies late into the night; now, though, we had less time to spend together as a couple, and the time we did have was constantly interrupted by some demand or need. And to be honest, I was lonely. We had entered parenthood on our own without a lot of support.

When I imagined becoming a mother for the first time, I never thought I would do it without my mom and dad. I thought they would be involved, the way they were with Matt's kids. My mom and I used to joke about how we would set up our life just like my orthodontist—a beautiful, successful woman who smelled like roses and who had two small children. Her own mother would take care of the children during the day and bring them to the office so they could all spend time together. My mom and I thought that was great, swearing that we would do the same thing one day. However, when my babies came, my mom was not around. I was alone in a strange new phase of life with no one to guide me or offer a nod of encouragement.

When I was first pregnant and my niece was still alive, I made a huge effort to work through things with my mom. Our relationship had deteriorated to almost nothing, but being pregnant made me want to look past all that so that my little girl would know her grandma. I called her up and begged her to be my mom again, telling her I was pregnant and scared and needed her. I couldn't believe I had been reduced to groveling.

She said she wanted to be there for me, but I had been so upset that she didn't know what I wanted her to do. I asked if we could meet to talk, and we made plans to meet at a Waffle House three hours away, halfway between our houses. Nervously, I sat across from her in a booth, trying to make her understand where I was coming from and what I needed from her. She was quiet, distant really. I could feel the thread that had connected us before was shredding, and the emptiness filled my chest with sorrow. She gave me some maternity clothes, still on disposable hangers in the plastic shopping bags, and we parted ways two hours later.

After my daughter was born, we tried to visit more often, but my parents were busy and my daughter screamed bloody murder every time she was strapped in the car seat. My mom offered her superficial small talk over the phone or email, sometimes relaying family gossip or a new recipe. I was grateful for this minimal connection, although it was insufficient in so many ways and the unresolved tension hovered constantly. Despite her saying everything was fine, it seemed clear that she was still angry at me for not going along and for creating such a division in our family.

The entire fallout was my fault because I was the one who pushed for an apology from Matt and Cheryl, unaware that I was issuing an ultimatum. I only wanted them to acknowledge my feelings or have an honest conversation; what I got instead was a years-long standoff. When my Uncle George passed away (another blow to our dwindling ranks), I decided I wanted to salvage what was left of my family. I swallowed my pride, let go of my own need to be seen, and offered them the apology I'd been waiting to receive. I sent emails and hand-written letters. Matt never responded and Derek offered a lukewarm acceptance. It was too little or too late because they never responded. I couldn't fix what was broken.

After my second child was born, my mom came to stay for two days. She was a perfect houseguest, folding laundry and tidying up. I longed to connect with her, the way we did when I was in high school and we'd have lunch together, but she insisted on staying out of the way.

One afternoon, I was rocking the baby to sleep in his room while my daughter napped. It was a rare moment of quiet, so I called my mom in to talk with me. I confessed that I was having a hard time caring for both a baby and a toddler by myself, that my anxiety was getting the better of me. I thought she would offer encouragement, maybe some advice. At the very least, I figured she would express some compassion. Instead, she said something I will never forget.

"You're exactly where I was when Samantha died."

I pressed her for more information, always eager to hear about Samantha, but she didn't offer much. She simply compared my anxious, exhausted state to her own during that time and left it at that. I have no idea what she meant by that, but for the next several months, I walked around paranoid that I would slip up and accidentally kill my child.

I could feel the irreparable rip in our connection, but I didn't understand it. I know they blamed me for everything, but I couldn't see how it was all my fault. Even if it was, my brothers had done all kinds of awful things over the years, and as far as I saw, they were never stonewalled.

Foolishly, I thought having a child might be a game changer because my mom had always put the grandchildren above any petty disputes. I had to keep quiet and make Cheryl happy for the sake of my nephews. My mom and dad refused to take my side in anything because it threatened their connection to my brother's children. I had to swallow my feelings at every turn for the sake of the kids. Yet I had children, and it didn't matter to any of them.

I couldn't wrap my head around it. My getting older didn't matter, my college and law degrees didn't matter, my fancy job didn't matter, my wedding didn't matter, my house didn't matter, my gifts didn't matter, my children didn't matter, and my efforts to show them how much I cared didn't matter. I gave them all the things I thought they wanted from me, fulfilling every obligation, but it meant nothing. They turned their backs on me.

It was then that I first started to wonder if maybe it wasn't that the things I accomplished didn't matter to them. Maybe it wasn't just because I had demanded an apology from Matt and Cheryl. Maybe it wasn't about any of the things I did or didn't do. Maybe it was simply because I didn't matter.

# Sixteen

When my kids were two and four, my husband and I were desperate for another change. We had been through a lot and were discouraged. We had lost our youthful optimism and needed to reclaim our passion. Determined to take our life by the reins, we decided to change our life. Again.

For several months, we wrote our dreams on posters we hung up around the house. We saved our money and evaluated our priorities, slowly narrowing in on our next move, ultimately deciding to start over in northern California. My husband left his job, and we established our own firm. Excited to start fresh, we set about building the life of our dreams. I was going to let go of my family problems and focus on my future.

It was incredibly exciting. We created a strategic plan for our business, and I picked out paint colors and artwork to hang in the kids' rooms and ordered a new couch to be delivered after we arrived. We made a list of all the adventures we would go on once we got there. The next chapter of our lives was going to be incredible.

The first several months in California were as spectacular as we hoped. We spent hours on the beach, collecting shells with our toes in the water. We walked along the cliffs and hiked in the redwoods. We found the local coffee place and sandwich spot, excited to make the community our home. We were high on the endless possibilities in front of us. Even the moving truck, filled with every item we owned, arriving four weeks late couldn't get us down. For just a moment, I forgot about the curse.

Then, after a few months, my anxiety came back with a vengeance, though I couldn't imagine what the problem was. My life was wonderful. By then, I had a happy marriage with two beautiful children, and we were living in a seaside community. I had attained the career goals I set for myself as a child and was settling into the next chapter of my life. I should have been perfectly content, but my body was signaling otherwise.

I felt like my heart was going to beat right out of my chest. I couldn't sit still. I busied myself with the tiniest of chores and panicked about the most mundane concerns: *Did I make that vet appointment yet? Why haven't I cleaned out that overstuffed linen closet? I better vacuum again because there are crumbs all over and I will just die if someone walks in and sees what a filthy mess this place is. Did I pay my annual bar dues? I was supposed to get those thank-you notes out last week!*

My brain was becoming a frantic emergency room for scabbed knees and quarter-size bruises, responding to the tiniest problems like they meant life or death. I was having a breakdown of epic proportions for no reason whatsoever, and that, I feared, meant I was going crazy. Looking back now, it was like every other moment of my life—just more exasperated.

It was the overwhelming feeling of being untethered to the world, adrift in a sea of pain and confusion that had no end, that finally propelled me into a therapist's office begging for some relief.

"So how about we start with your body? How does it feel?"

The absurdity of this question seemed obvious to me at the time. Why did I come to a therapist for my rapidly decaying mental health if I wanted to talk about my body? I clearly must not have understood what she was asking.

"Do you feel tightness anywhere? Do you feel cold or hot? Do you have any physical sensations in a particular area more than in others?"

I inhaled deeply through my nose, unsure what my breath would expel. "I don't feel anything."

"Do you feel numb?"

"Actually, yes," I said. "Like the dentist just gave me a shot of Novocain."

"Is there anything else? How do your shoulders feel?"

"Tight and raised," I responded. "They keep creeping up to my ears."

"How about your chest or your stomach?"

"Nothing, really. Well, my stomach always feels twisted into knots."

"How about your legs?"

"Very tight, squeezed together actually," I said. "It's like I have a small ball wedged in between them and my thighs are squeezing together to hold it in place. Except my thighs feel like they're lifting up, up, up."

"It sounds like your body is trying to tell us something. It seems like it's afraid. Do you feel afraid?"

"No."

"Have you felt this kind of physical sensation before?"

"Only all the time!" I exclaimed. "When I'm flipped off by a random stranger on the freeway. When I sit on the crinkled paper lining on the doctor's examination table. When I dial the phone number for my parents."

"Sometimes your body will feel numb in an attempt to protect you from some kind of emotion or feeling. What do you think is underneath the numbness?"

Until that afternoon in late September, I was oblivious to the depth of my own deception. For the next three months, I attempted to explain my relationship with my family to my therapist, but I couldn't figure out how to convey something so intangible. Every time I tried to anchor the truth down with a word or a phrase, it wriggled out of place and left me mumbling. As I spoke, I felt my words fall onto the floor without the meaning I intended to attach to them. It was excruciating.

"I'm going crazy," I would say.

My therapist would calmly remind me that my sanity was intact, at least for the moment. "There is no sign of that. I think you are feeling overwhelmed and disoriented."

"I just don't understand," I said. "I love my life. I have a wonderful husband and beautiful children. I live in a beautiful place and we have enough money. What's the problem?"

"Well, that is what we are trying to figure out together."

# The Chrysalis

*When the caterpillar reaches its fullest capacity, it forms itself into a chrysalis where it begins a remarkable transformation. The caterpillar undergoes a complete metamorphosis, where the old caterpillar body is broken down into imaginal cells where many, but not all, of the cells are destroyed as the new butterfly form comes into being.*

# Seventeen

One day, on my way home from a particularly unsettling therapy session, I was seized by an emotional deluge that hit me with such force I could barely drive. My hands shook violently, and I had barely enough strength to keep my foot on the gas. My eyesight was blurry from the puddle of tears that persisted no matter how many times I blinked. Nothing infiltrated my daze, not the cars beside me or the radio that was probably playing in the background.

One after another, memories hit me like artillery fire. Visions of the pendant light in my bedroom and the smell of alcohol. The bright red stains on my white bathing suit. My fearful footsteps on the textured linoleum of the bathroom. My flannel nightgown. Pain.

I was out of my mind by the time I pulled into our driveway, stumbling through the door and finally collapsing on my knees in our bedroom. When Will found me, our two young children running behind him, I told him to take the kids next door. As he ran out of the bedroom, I could hear my son calling, "No, I want Mommy!"

At that point, my whole body began to convulse as I wrapped my arms across my chest and huddled on my knees by the foot of our bed. My head throbbed as if it was being pounded against the wall over and over again. *Thud, thud, thud, thud, thud.* I heard a ringing sound in my ears, like a high-pitched cry that would not stop. I wanted to peel my face off, to unzip myself from the experience I was trapped inside. Unable to find a way out, I sobbed hysterically, rocking myself back and forth.

"What happened?" I heard my husband's voice as he slipped his arm around my shoulders and sat on the ground next to me.

"Something's wrong," I said, crying harder as the muscles in my face tried to hold in the pain ... or maybe hold back the realizations falling like a string of dominos.

I didn't want to tell my husband about the cascade of memories that followed me home, shaking loose, one after another, from somewhere deep inside and ricocheting inside my head. Vague, heavy, somatic. I felt caught in a whirlwind of memories and pain and fear and shock and all I wanted was for it to stop. I truly thought I was going crazy. From the way I looked and sounded, I think my husband probably feared that I already was.

"It's okay. Everything's going to be alright," he said, rubbing my back. "Just breathe."

I buried my face in my hands and bawled. For over an hour I couldn't do anything but wail, then weep, then whimper under the watchful eyes of my loving husband. I melted into the shag carpet of our bedroom, lying there, unable to lift my head or wipe the tears and snot that dribbled all over my face. I was drowning.

Living with a history of childhood sexual abuse is a lot like climbing a mountain, feeling the crumbling earth beneath your feet as you trudge uphill with all your might. The only thing keeping you steady and upright is the forward momentum. Leaning forward, your eyes turned to God, you feel like you have a chance.

You're terrified of turning around because to turn around is to face the fragility of your own existence. Having been unable to protect yourself, you are at the mercy of someone who has forced past your boundaries to brutally invade your innermost sanctuary. Acknowledging that reality forces you to acknowledge that evil is real and lurks in the most unlikely places. It destroys your innocence and challenges the idea that your life matters to anyone, even God. As a child, and then as an adult, you somehow know that facing these things will make you stumble and fall down into the deep, dark pit you always feared was waiting for you.

The problem is if you want to heal, you have to turn around because behind you are the pieces of yourself that were discarded or stolen along the way, and you need them. You need them to make sense of the journey you've been on and the person you've become because of it. Otherwise, you walk around the world lost, searching for something you didn't know existed because it left you before you could properly claim it as your own. You have to face the deep, dark pit. I not only faced that pit, I fell into it headfirst.

Once the first memories came untethered and invaded my reality, others followed. Usually, a wave of chilling tranquility would wash over me, literally freezing me in my tracks; I couldn't move or even blink. It was a familiar daze, a sedative of detachment. I would force myself to feel the wind brush against my cheeks. I'd strain to hear the sounds of cars rushing past and birds chirping nearby. I'd squeeze my hands into fists until I could feel the pain of my fingernails digging into my palms. Then I would remind myself that I was safe in this moment, and although small and insignificant, I was okay. I said those words over and over again, even if I didn't believe them.

Then I would be instantly transported back to another time...

*My back's against the wall as dishes fly across the kitchen, my parents screaming madly. My normally passive, shy father lashes out in a blind rage, his eyes narrowed and menacing. As if to match pitches with him, my mother shrieks in a drunken slur, her body flailing about madly. I feel myself trying to run out into the fray, but Derek's arm thrusts into my stomach like a railroad crossing gate.*

I'd become encapsulated by the terror of a moment until it was finished with me. Sometimes what I recalled was foggy, but familiar—like a dream I'd had many times before. Other times the memory seemed to come from the deepest recesses of my mind, appearing like an apparition that was hard to fully grasp with all my senses. Afterwards, I would come back to my present self, exhausted and confused.

Memories with images were tough to handle, but those my mind didn't record in that manner were far worse. The most horrific memories were merely fragments of feelings, smells, sounds, bodily responses, and an eerie knowing of exactly what was happening. With no video recall and a lifetime of seeing my family through rose-colored glasses, I couldn't believe what

I was remembering, what I knew but refused to believe. It was too outrageous to be true.

Yet I knew it was. I don't know how or why, but a part of me was absolutely clear that something happened to me. Even if I had the details mixed up, the fact that I was sexually abused was just that—a fact. It was not up for debate.

# Eighteen

Being sexually abused—the part that gets everyone's attention—wasn't the worst part of remembering. It was one grain of sand trapped in the bottom of an hourglass, one of many tragic moments that steadily flowed through a tiny pathway from my subconscious into my awareness until, surprisingly, there were no more. No explanations, no illuminating histories, nothing to account for the disastrous degradation of a family. Nothing to justify the emptiness surrounding me. All that surfaced with the abuse was the apathy and fear and pain and cowardice and numbness that allowed for such an atrocity against my young soul in the first place, robbing me of any solace that was not of my own making.

Unable to defend myself or run away, I played dead in order to survive the ordeal, and with great mercy, my mind syphoned off the traumatic memory of what had happened so that I could get on with living. I suppose nothing else could have been done back then. At least there wasn't anything a five-year-old girl could do for herself, except to find shelter within the intricate confines of her psyche … taking out a payday loan that would not come due for many, many years.

The mind is a fickle friend in times of distress. It can contort what the eyes perceive. It can override our nervous system's sirens. More importantly, it can create a fiction more palatable than fact and an explanation more satisfying than truth. My mind invented a beautiful fairy tale wherein I was the beloved fairy princess, but that's all it was. A fairy tale. A big pretend. I don't blame my mind though. I think it did what it had to do to survive.

It's impossible to describe the kind of primal fear that takes hold of you when your life is threatened by the very people you thought were supposed to protect it. As children, we are trusting and loyal without any reservation. All our eggs are in one basket. In that moment, when the person you love most in the world transforms into the monster you were assured did not live under your bed, the whole world stops. You are keenly aware, even as a child, that you are moments away from extinguishment. You are utterly defenseless, and in that moment of complete domination, your soul squares off with defeat.

Yet your longing, your adoration, your pure obsession with those who facilitated life does not subside. It burns brighter, a white-hot flame of childish need that blocks out anything that threatens it. This need is all that matters. Indisputable facts and inconvenient questions vanish in its blinding glow, creating a protective haven. The denial serves as an opiate, dulling the pain and rendering the truth soft and malleable. This need is what enables us to make sense of the senseless, to understand what our young minds are incapable of fathoming. Fueled by its irrational urgency, all we know is that we need to be loved and protected to survive—and survive we must. So we trust the liars, and we betray ourselves in order to belong.

Until that point, my deception had shielded me from my family's hatred and apathy that suddenly rushed out like military troops sent to destroy my world. My deception had been a hard, protective coating that insulated me from the anguish I now felt, from the despair crushing my soul. I wanted to run or fight or disappear when my childhood armor dissolved, leaving me exposed and raw, but I knew those tactics were insufficient. I couldn't outrun my own body or fight the shadows lurking in my head.

I had opened Pandora's box. No matter how hard I tried, I could not capture its contents and put them back inside. I had no choice but to surrender to the ugliness of my life as it tumbled out in fits of urgency. I was bombarded with images, sounds, smells, and even tastes that sparked new, terrible realizations. And all I could do was endure.

# Nineteen

In a dystopian movie called *The Truman Show*, Jim Carrey plays Truman Burbank, a man who is adopted and raised by a corporation inside a simulated television show revolving around his life. He doesn't know anything different, so he goes about his contrived life happily for many years until he starts noticing unusual events, like a spotlight falling out of the sky.

As Truman becomes more and more suspicious about his "reality," the show goes to great efforts to control his mind so that he continues playing his role. Nevertheless, he grows more convinced that something is wrong and finally tries to escape by boat. The show tries to stop him in every possible way, but he persists and eventually reaches an exit door. Unable to contrive any further obstacles, the show's creator acknowledges that he is in an artificial reality show, then he urges Truman to stay, telling him that there is no more truth in the real world and that, by staying in his artificial world, he would have nothing to fear. Truman, consumed with great despair, leaves, his fate wholly unknown.

I think my life has unfolded much like *The Truman Show*. My childhood reality was created entirely by my family, and their artificial world governed many of my adult years. For a long time, I was completely unaware that a different reality existed. The moment I began considering other possibilities, however, I became suspicious. Stories suddenly didn't add up. Words didn't match actions. Hypocrisy and double standards went unchallenged. Feelings were labeled unreliable and harmful.

Like Truman, I knew something was wrong, that there was more to my story than what was presented to me. I could feel it, even though I didn't understand it. I fought with my brothers, begging for attention and love that I was told I already had. I worked hard to please everyone, eager to gain a drop of their approval. I took care of everyone in the hopes that I would be needed, if not wanted. I did everything I could to earn my family's love, which I was assured existed even though I couldn't feel it. Like Truman, I was suspicious, and I pushed for answers as to what actually constituted my "reality."

Of course, my family sought to control my suspicions. Whenever I asked questions or pointed out inconsistencies, I was hushed, shamed, ridiculed, and bullied into going along. They lied to me. They contradicted, shamed, humiliated, and questioned me. They yelled at me, guilt-tripped me, and flat-out ignored my attempts to understand the truth. They talked me in circles until I was dizzy with shame and confusion and all too eager to submit to their assertions just so I could make it all stop. When all else failed, they ostracized me.

Their preferred tactic was distraction. Growing up, there was always drama in my family. Among our extended family, aunts and uncles, my brothers and their wives, we always had a crisis on our hands, a crisis that affected everyone else way more than me. Even if we were all mourning the same person, I was considered the least impacted—if I was considered at all. If I had the nerve to point that out, a concerted effort was made to knock me down a peg or two.

It was essential that I never got too big for my britches. If I became too audacious or proud, they would chip away at my confidence. My brothers, especially, would demean me, criticize me, and be downright cruel just to put me in my place. Meek, insecure, and timid defined my place.

I remember getting dressed for a high school event and coming out into the living room, beaming proudly in my new dress. Derek snickered and then proceeded to lead the family in a laughing fit of hysterics—sound effects, finger guns, and all—over how my new, perky boobs looked like torpedoes. By the time the doorbell rang, I ran to greet my sixteen-year-old date with my sweater buttoned up to my chin and my hands crossed in front of my two hilarious weapons.

I could never make sense of how they could mistreat and ignore me in big and small ways, then insist I was the favorite. They would yell at me and tell me I was a selfish, sharp-tongued brat, but then say they didn't have any problems with me. It didn't make any sense to me then, and when my memories had emerged, things made even less sense. I was a real-life Truman Burbank, sensing and seeing inconsistencies all around me that told a very different story from the one I knew.

Until my memories surfaced, I was unable and unwilling to see the reality of my family, the one that existed beyond the sanitized, redacted version. I dismissed anything inconsistent with them being the loving family I needed them to be, but in one fell swoop, this deluge of memories upended my entire world and forced me to see what I didn't want to see.

# Twenty

My memories were so vivid, and my body reacted to them in such telling ways. It routinely went numb whenever I talked about my past, sometimes powering itself down into a state of paralysis mid-conversation. For three weeks after my first memory emerged, I spontaneously bled for three weeks straight. One of the most upsetting physical reactions I had was the way arousal mixed with shame and intrusive memories. Sometimes when my emotions spiked, I would fall asleep midday without warning.

In keeping with my personality, I went in search of information to help explain what was happening to me. I devoured books, research papers, and online articles about recovered memories, brain development, trauma, alcoholism, abuse, and anything that seemed pertinent to my experience. I joined online support groups and poured through the heartbreaking stories of other survivors who were also trudging up the hill towards healing.

Every book I devoured on the subject supported my body's recollection, rather than my disbelieving mind. Books and research papers offered tangible evidence and theories to support what I was undergoing, providing a framework to contain what was happening. Every sensation I had mirrored sensations other abuse victims had experienced—and our stories were more similar than they were different. I was turning out to be a textbook example of somatic reexperiencing, and I was not happy about it.

Despite feeling like a teenager again, wanting it all to just go away, I couldn't help myself from ruminating over my childhood—the things that happened, the people in it, everything. There was such an enormous gap in between what I believed about my life and the reality of what I was experiencing, and it was hard to connect them. I went from one extreme to the other within seconds, depending on what information I let into my head.

I had always believed that I was raised in a loving family who thought the world of me. I was their baby girl, their shining star. They loved me so much. They couldn't have done something bad to me—or allowed something bad to be done to me—because they loved me. Clearly, I was certifiably insane to think they had abused me.

Yet, my body had opened my eyes to an entirely different reality. My body's signals and my memories were clear. I had been abused, and that fact was inconstant with any belief that my family loved me. Without any thread connecting these two opposing perspectives, I took turns between them. That meant I took turns being two separate people, which effectively, meant I had a split personality. At least that's how it felt.

I needed the truth so that I could go back to being one person—one sane person. I couldn't trust myself to know what the truth was, and even if I could, which self should I trust? The one who knew I was abused or the one who knew my family would never do that to me? I had deceived myself for decades by dissociating these experiences to the point of forgetting them entirely. How could I believe that my memories were truthful? At that point, I was convinced that the only way I could move on was to contact my family and ask them for the truth.

After dropping my kids off at preschool one morning, I pulled into a Target parking lot near my house and parked near the back. Holding my phone with shaking hands, I found my parents' number. My index finger hovered over those digits for a few moments as my stomach churned. I felt faint.

I put the phone down and looked out the window, uselessly trying to calm my nerves. My forehead was clammy and my jaw was clenched. I told myself I didn't have to do it. I didn't have to call. I was already not speaking to my folks as it was, so I could just continue on in the silence. There was still time to safely retreat from this kamikaze mission.

Then I dialed.

My mom answered the phone and, within seconds, sensed that something was wrong. Her tone immediately shifted from casually upbeat to defensively rigid.

"What can I do for you?"

"What happened to me when I was little?"

Stunned silence hung between us for only a second, but that second seemed to go on forever and ever as I felt the sting of its affirmation.

"What? What are you talking about? Nothing happened to you when you were little."

Her words lilted with false casualness, but I could hear the tension in them sputtering nervously from her clenched jaw. I could feel her growing rage seeping through the phone.

"I know, Mom. I know."

"I don't know what you're talking about. I don't know what you want me to tell you."

I listed out three events in my life, laying them out like breadcrumbs she could follow to the conclusion I had already formed. My hope was that I could lead her to it without having to say it out loud. I wasn't ready to talk about it directly. I just needed to know I wasn't having a psychotic break—at least that's what I thought at the time—so I proceeded to ask about those three telltale moments in my life.

She lied about every single one. Every one. She denied events I lived through and recorded with my active memory. She refused to admit to seemingly inconsequential events from the past. Things I experienced firsthand, she said never happened. I could not fathom why my own mother would lie to me about things she knew to be true. I wasn't prepared for that. I hadn't even brought up the abuse, but she was already battening down the hatches and preparing for battle.

I had no idea what to do then, so I hung up and sobbed for twenty minutes in the front seat of my car, avoiding the concerned glances of passing drivers. Then I wiped my face and drove home.

Later that night, she called and left a message. In her sweetest singsong voice, she said she just needed time to get her head together. I had caught her off guard, that was all. If I wanted to talk, she would answer any questions I wanted to ask. I couldn't pick up the phone fast enough.

The world stopped for a split second as I waited for her to answer. I had absolutely no idea what she was about to say, but I knew it would be the piece of the puzzle I was missing. I knew that my life was going to start making more sense. I was finally going to understand why I was such a misfit, why I had so many misplaced emotions and physical responses, and why I was having a mental breakdown. I was about to learn the truth.

The phone rang on and on, a sign that she was on the other line. I looked at the clock and realized it was almost midnight where she lived. Who could she be talking to so late at night, especially after leaving me a message about something so incredibly important? I hung up and tried calling again, waiting even longer as it rang and rang, my hands shaking as my stomach dropped. And then she answered.

"Who were you talking to?"

"Nobody."

"Mom …"

"I wasn't talking to anyone."

"Mom, I can tell when you're on the other line. You took forever to click over."

She paused for one excruciatingly long second. "I was talking to Matt, my son who loves me, if you really want to know."

Her words sucker-punched the air right out of me. Why in the world would she be talking to Matt right now? I began stammering, trying to get my bearings.

"Tell me what happened when I was little."

"Nothing happened."

"Mom …"

"Who've you been talking to?"

I was dumbfounded by her reaction. She didn't ask what I was talking about or express any concern about why I believed something happened to me. She didn't show any curiosity as to what I wanted to know or why. She just matter-of-factly insisted that nothing happened. Then, she immediately wanted to know who I was talking to, as if someone had put ideas into my head. What happened to her being willing to answer any questions I had? Why was she responding this way?

Our conversation went off the rails after that. She oscillated from accusing family members of making mob-like threats to questioning me about what psychedelic drugs I had taken. *Who put these ideas into your head? Where is this coming from?* Then she said something that haunts me to this day.

"You know what I think? I think you just don't like me very much. Well, you know what? I don't like you either."

# Twenty-One

For a long time, my mother was my hero. She was beautiful, funny, and perfect at everything she did. Her home was always nice and clean, her meals were homemade goodness, and her checkbook was always balanced. She was crafty, making costumes and all kinds of décor. She could put together batches of chili for the boosters to sell at football games and prepare a holiday feast that would rival the Pioneer Woman's best. My mom wrapped a gift so beautifully that you wouldn't want to open it, but since she bought the most wonderful presents, you would force yourself to rip it apart anyway.

When I was a teenager, I would do errands with my mom and afterwards we would stop somewhere for a burger and fries. I would talk her ear off while nibbling on french fries, eager to connect with her about any topic under the sun. We talked about friends, family, work, and school. It didn't matter what our conversation entailed, just that we were spending time together. I longed to feel close to her, and those conversations were everything to me.

I never had the same tendency to romanticize my father. His

emotionally detached demeanor made it hard to gather evidence of his perfection. I was satisfied, for the most part, thinking that he was a quiet, hardworking man who wanted only the best for his family. I knew that to be true, not only from my own experience, but from the constant assertions of my mother, who took it upon herself to be my father's public relations representative, interpreting his absence and giving words to his silence. It was as if marriage fused them into one human, and my mom was the spokesperson for their union. In that way, I suppose I either worshipped or criticized my father, depending on my mother's proxy. Whatever she said had to be true and right and just—because she said it.

This perfect image of my mother became harder to protect once my memories broke loose. As I reflected on my childhood, moments came to mind that didn't fit into this ideal version of my mother. Like the stories of my grandparents and other relatives, the less glamorous truths were kept at bay. Had I ever wanted to recall them, which I didn't, I could have done so instantly. However, these stories presented inconvenient contradictions that threatened to disprove my theory that my mom was the most perfect woman alive. So I guess I ignored them.

It was a well-known fact that my parents drank when I was very little. Everyone did, and they were no exceptions. Pop culture—with its steady emphasis on drunken hilarity, commercials with frogs and horses, and sexy girls drinking pink cosmos—only strengthened my conviction that drinking was a very normal part of being a grown-up. DARE didn't shake my perception because drugs were the problem, not alcohol. However, when Grandma Betty passed away and her drinking problem came out, my eyes were opened to the idea that drinking could be a cause for concern. My mom joined everyone else in casting judgment against my grandma, which made me think that people who couldn't handle their liquor were weak. Since my parents could handle it just fine, I felt reassured that it wasn't a problem for them.

But that wasn't true at all. Even with my splotchy memory, I vividly remember my parents getting into knock-down, drag-out fights when they were drunk. It didn't happen all the time, at least that I recall, but it happened enough. I don't have many memories of it, only a few that offer a terrifying glimpse into the tumultuousness of those days. My body contains most of my memories, and they come in the form of chills along my spine or a sudden outbreak of sweat the moment I'm near a loud, raucous drunk, especially if that drunk puts a hand on me.

My cousin once confided in me that, when she stayed with us, my father sometimes became really violent when he drank, sparring with my mom and focusing his rage on Derek. Terrified, my cousin would drag Matt out to the front lawn for safety. When I asked her where I was during all of this, she said I was left alone in my crib. She also said I became ridiculously good at crawling out of it well before I turned one year old. I guess I learned to look after myself early on.

It was around that time that Derek, labeled the troublemaker, reportedly ran away and hid out with his girlfriend's family. He told them my parents were alcoholics, which hurt my parents deeply—not so much because it was true, but because he had aired our dirty laundry to an outsider. At some point, he was dragged back home by a well-meaning priest, and the story became a funny nod to my brother's rebellious antics. In telling this story, my mom erased any legitimate problems stemming from their drinking that could have warranted my brother running away and left it as a story of how teenage rebellion broke a mother's heart.

When I was in elementary school, probably around eight years old, my parents abruptly stopped drinking. Nobody ever mentioned why, although I now have my suspicions. They never went to Alcoholics Anonymous or anything like that. Just as my dad had stopped smoking, they merely swore off the stuff and never touched it for years. Nobody talked to me about why they stopped or the importance of being sober, except Matt once shared that alcoholism could be inherited, so I should always be careful. His warning scared me at first, but within a couple years he was drinking Grey Goose and joining in the fun, so I brushed it off as yet another thing I wouldn't understand until I was older.

As I settled into high school, my parents slowly slid back into drinking again—one glass of wine here, a vodka drink there. It was mostly on the weekends, and they seemed to enjoy it, laughing and carrying on, seeming more like carefree teenagers than me. Sometimes I worried about them, but it wasn't my place to be concerned. As bold as I was becoming, I knew I couldn't question them on this issue. They were adults, and they could choose to have a drink or two if they wanted. Plus, they didn't have a problem, so I was assured it was okay.

Toward the end of high school and into college, alcohol was always flowing when my family got together. It started out social and sometimes stayed that way. Other times, it teetered on the edge of chaos. My mom would start out giggling and happy, but after a few more drinks, she would yell and carry on about a problem she had with someone. She'd lay it all out, slurring and usually repeating herself a few times. Then the past would resurrect itself as grievances were aired, and awful things were said.

My brothers seemed to enjoy watching her spiral out of control, practically laughing at her inebriated folly. It hurt my heart to see her so fragile and vulnerable, which stood in stark contrast to my brothers' apathy toward her in those moments. Mom would eventually become incoherent, and I would drag her away from the discussion protectively, leading her to her bedroom and tucking her into bed. The next morning was business as usual.

These moments in time, along with the facts and truths they conveyed, were like books stacked on a shelf. They were always there, ready to be looked at, but I relegated them to the background until they became of no consequence. For so long, I refused to face them because they didn't fit into the ideal image I had constructed of my mother. I needed her to be perfect.

In my quest for the truth, however, I couldn't pick and choose what facts to let in. It was an all-or-nothing proposition. I needed to know who I was in my entirety, which meant I needed to know my parents in their entirety. I had to figure out how to fit these moments—and how they reflected their character—into my perception of them. As I did, my mom morphed from an impossible goddess into a significantly flawed human.

It wasn't an easy transition to make. The mother I thought I had didn't exist, and the one I did have was not living up to my standards, let alone the rest of the world's. I reasoned that no one is perfect, and it was totally normal for a grown daughter to stop idealizing her mother. She didn't have to be perfect to have been a great mom. So what if she had her faults? Don't we all? The important thing was that she loved me. As long as she loved me, I could handle the rest.

I had always been desperate for her love, yet it seemed like she never had enough left over for me. She was always busy with work or dinner preparations. She had to deal with the incessant stream of crises that plagued our family. She needed to rest or take a bath. To get her attention, my needs were required to rise to the level of an emergency, and I didn't want to be another burden. So I settled for the space between.

In elementary school, I would get home two hours before my mom returned home from work. Too lonesome inside the house, I would often sit with my dog, Samson, in the open garage finishing my homework and watching for her red Chevy to pull into the driveway. If it was fall, I would watch as a burst of Santa Ana winds sent a cluster of brittle, yellow leaves swirling through the air. Sometimes tumbleweeds rolled down the street or a few big drops of rain fell on the cement driveway. It was times like these when I felt so alone, so abandoned by the world at the young age of eleven, that I would remind myself that I had the best mother in the whole world.

I suppose I needed to see my mother as a supernatural being, unhindered by human limitations. My fragile self-esteem needed to look past her underhanded remarks about how I was an ugly duckling or big-boned. I had to believe she meant well when she told me my brother was smart, but I made up for my lesser intelligence by being a hard worker. With my dad either at work or emotionally distant, and my brothers being significantly older and unconcerned with me, I needed someone to love, and I needed to believe someone loved me.

After that night on the phone, however, I wasn't sure she ever loved me. She certainly didn't like me—she said as much. As I let myself wonder about her true feelings for me, I felt the final brick shake loose, dismantling that pedestal I had her on.

# Twenty-Two

Delusion is the last line of defense before disillusionment. When the truth is too awful to face, or too entrenched to rally against, we have to find a way to avoid the vast darkness of hopelessness. We need to hang on to the ideas of goodness and possibility, even if they are nowhere to be found. That way, we can one day set off in the direction of claiming them for ourselves.

Delusion is born out of hope. We hope that things aren't so bad. We hope that what we know happened didn't actually happen. We hope that with enough love, enough determination and healing, we can one day fix what is broken. We clutch this hope to our hearts like a security blanket, a tattered consolation of our own making, the comfort of "one day" so deliciously soothing that there is no worse torture than ripping it from our clutches. So even as the thread connecting us to our families, our histories, and even our sanity begins to fray, we hope.

Rewriting our stories is one of the most powerful survival mechanisms I know, and it is fueled by hope. By creatively tweaking our narrative, we give birth to the kind of world we want to live in. We define what we want for ourselves, rather than settling for what we've got, charting our course toward what we desperately need to be real. We read into actions and events, imbuing them with meaning that isn't necessarily there. We delude ourselves into believing what we want to believe, what we need to believe, in order to survive.

After confronting my mom, my delusions began to disintegrate. Having directly faced off with my mother's shadow side, I couldn't deny she had one any longer. I began to realize that I had deluded myself in so many ways, from believing my mother was an infallible goddess to believing that my father would protect me.

When I was in high school, I didn't have a curfew. I was told to be responsible, but I was not given a time to be home or any strict rules about where I could and could not go. It was a teenager's dream to be able to come and go of their own accord, but I wasn't just any teenager. When I was out with friends—friends whose parents were strict and exacting about their whereabouts—I lied and told them I had a curfew, lamenting my father's overprotective nature, complaining about how he treated me like a child. I even roped in my brothers, asserting that they were constantly shielding me, priding themselves on my sheltered naiveté.

When boys came to the door, I ushered them into the living room for the dreaded introduction to my intimidating father, who merely shook their hands affably and sent us on our way. After the front door closed behind us, I would gush about how much my dad must have liked them to let them off so easily. Later, my husband engaged in the same song and dance. After a lot of buildup on my part, he nervously asked permission to marry me, and my father shrugged. *I like you, her mother likes you, and now I don't have to worry about her anymore.*

I needed my family to be protective of me to feel safe. For so long, I had watched them rally around family members and shut the world out in defense of them. My family lived by the rule that we could say awful things to one another, but an outsider better not dare cross one of us. That was their way of showing love and affection. I reasoned that I never experienced this kind of fierce defensiveness because I never needed it. I did all I could to avoid disasters, desperate to be pleasing and successful to earn their approval. On top of that, someone was always saying, "Just wait 'til life knocks you down a few pegs," which terrified me. Still, I knew that my family was waiting in the wings should I ever need them.

My belief in their love and protection was enough to propel me forward with the confidence I needed to withstand the forces of the world. My delusion was a saving grace, lifting me above the confines of reality. I could attend college far away from home, embark on a difficult career path, and risk everything to chase my dreams because I had a safety net. Believing that my parents and brothers would drop everything to help me, just the way I so often did for them, was everything to me. If the world messed with me, they would come to my defense. If the world knocked me down, they would pick me back up. However, believing something to be true doesn't make it so.

Without the filter of delusion, I had to see my relationship with them as it really was. In reflecting on the biggest moments of my life, I felt a lot like the elephant Dumbo soaring through the air, suddenly realizing that the magic feather wasn't magic at all.

When I broke up with Kyle, my high school sweetheart of four years, I handled it alone. Having shared such a powerful, intimate connection with him for years, I was devastated beyond reason. Losing him was one of the hardest things I've ever gone through, but my family didn't offer much comfort during that time. It was just a breakup, after all. I had to comfort myself, and I found a great deal of solace in the idea that we would meet up again years down the road, happy to see how our separate lives turned out. I always imagined that we would come back together and share a sweet reunion, much like the one Garth Brooks sings about in "Unanswered Prayers."

Before we got to have that moment, though, Kyle died. Three years after we broke up, at just twenty-six, he was tragically killed by a roadside bomb in Iraq, leaving behind a wife and a baby girl. His death hit me like a ton of bricks. I was devasted in ways I never could have anticipated. Will, my husband of exactly one year, was just as surprised at my seemingly misplaced grief. I worried that I hadn't really dealt with our breakup as much as I had avoided it, and I feared what that might mean for my marriage.

Because Kyle had been around since I was seventeen years old, I turned to my family for support. They had celebrated holidays with him, invited him on vacation, and watched him transform from a child into a man. They knew him and how much I had loved him. They might appreciate what he meant to me, and why it was so devastating to know he was never coming back. His little girl would never know him like I did. His wife would never have another anniversary or another birthday with him. He would never light up the world again with his smile. I hoped my family would understand how painful this loss was for me.

My parents came to his funeral with me and my husband, but they said very little. The most I got from them was my mom saying, *He was like a son to me.* They seemed more concerned with reading the paper and talking about the weather than supporting me. Since I was the ex-girlfriend, it was incredibly awkward being at his funeral in the first place. Then when I sobbed like a baby in front of a crowd of mourning strangers, it seemed so much worse.

My husband stayed by my side and carried me through it. He was my rock, steadying me through my grief over the loss of the man he replaced. I didn't want to lean on him, but there was no one else to keep me upright. My parents stood only a few feet away, unable or unwilling to support me through my devastation.

Hours later, I sat in a restaurant booth across from my parents. As we recounted the tear-filled eulogy, the tiny American flags in everyone's hands, and the three-volley salute echoing through the cemetery while his little girl frolicked innocently at his gravesite, I wondered if they didn't notice how deep his death cut me. Maybe I was too good at putting on a strong face, and they couldn't see I was falling apart. But too much heartache, too many tears, and too little sleep left me deflated to the point of barely being able to carry on a conversation. I was a body stripped of a soul. Anyone could see that, even my parents.

As my husband drove the six hours back to our home, I reclined in the passenger seat. My eyelids refused to stay open, trapping me inside my head with all my sorrow. I couldn't understand why his death hit me so hard, but there was no mistaking that it did.

Thinking my military brother would understand this kind of unique loss, I reached out to Derek. Maybe it was a military thing, I thought. Since he had served in the Marines, maybe he would better understand. He had seen a lot in his fifteen years of service. When I told him what happened, he said he was sorry, his voice aloof, callous even. He grew quiet, and I asked him to say something—anything. *What do you want me to tell you?* Years later during an argument, he blamed me for not even telling him about Kyle's death, and my mind exploded with the memory of him offering me nothing while I cried over the phone.

As I revisited those moments after his passing, without the veil of my delusion, I finally understood why my grief was so profound. Kyle was not just an ex-boyfriend. He was the first person who gave me the courage to love myself. He came along at just the right time to save me from the dark pit of loneliness and despair that was threatening to swallow me whole, the one I denied even existed back then. His love emboldened me to fight for my soul, a battle I wouldn't understand I was fighting until my memories unleashed themselves a decade later. I was grieving one of the most important people in my life, but my family didn't really support me through it.

I've moved across the country, lost my job, struggled to conceive, gone through serious health scares with my children and myself, and suffered all kinds of bumps and bruises through the years, and none of those experiences warranted my family showing up for me. Time after time, I faced hardship, even my own mortality, but it has never been enough to warrant their attention.

That's not how they saw it. They thought I was too sensitive, too emotional, too needy, that I expected too much. They couldn't understand what in the world I wanted from them, demanding a list detailing my expectations. When I brought up the sacrifices I made for them through the years (to show them examples of how I wanted them to be there for me), they said I was throwing it in their faces. My efforts to state my boundaries and take some space resulted in my brothers leaving twelve voicemails overnight, calling me a bitch and telling me to stop running away like a child. Not once did they every respond to me with genuine care or concern, or even curiosity. Their response was rote and predictably defensive, no matter what I said.

Looking at these moments clearly was painful and blinding, like staring at the sun. It had been easier to believe their lies. I could believe that I was too needy and ask for less. I could reduce my expectations to the point of having none. I could keep asking for what I needed in clear, direct ways, believing them when they said they just didn't understand. I could even be grateful that my life was so easy and charmed that help and support were unnecessary. I would rather be a contortionist, squeezing into every possible position, just to avoid seeing the truth—that the caring family I thought I had was my own fabricated delusion.

# Twenty-Three

Being fourteen years older than me, Derek has always been just out of my reach. We didn't grow up together. By the time we moved, he had already joined the Marines and moved out. Even though I was only four, I was the one who first recognized him after basic training, his long hair shaved into a crew cut and his body sculpted into a soldier.

He spent long periods away from us, but when he came home, I was the first one to wrap my arms around him. I would wait anxiously by the window, watching for him. Our new house didn't have a bedroom for him, so he and his buddies crashed on the living room couch when they visited and I got to deliver the blankets and pillows. I waited on them with pride, happy to earn their compliments.

Not long after joining the military, Derek married his high school sweetheart, Lori. They settled down, bought a place of their own, and got a dog. Suddenly, we began making trips to visit them, rather than waiting up all night to see his bright red truck pull into the driveway. This separation solidified his status as an adult in my eyes, and made him seem less like my sibling and more like my cool uncle who visited a lot.

Derek was the definition of cool in my book. He was athletic, funny, and the subject of every outrageous adventure story my family told. When he was around, the whole room lit up with laughter and fun. Even though I was little and unable to truly participate in most conversations, I saturated myself in the warmth and vibrancy of his voice. There was something magnetic about his personality, and I wanted to be around him all of the time. But the visits we had with him were few and far between, and it was never enough. I always wanted more.

I suppose I was starving for attention, especially from a father figure. My dad was always at a distance from me, and the world. No matter how much I pushed him, he never engaged with me the way I wanted. He shut me out. Since Matt was either hateful or apathetic towards me, that left only Derek to fill the void. His physical absence should have ruled him out as a candidate, but it also allowed a lot of room for my imagination to build him up as someone larger than life.

I began to fantasize about him being my proud, protective hero. As a Marine, his job was to protect people, and deep down, I wanted someone to protect me. I wanted someone to think I was valuable enough to deserve safeguarding. Since he was never around to contradict my view of him, this fantasy entrenched itself into my psyche. As a result, I grew up longing for him the way a princess trapped in a castle longs for a knight in shining armor. I knew, in time, he would come for me.

My hope that he would one day transform into my hero persisted, even after he took great care to demolish it. He's always had a knack for purposefully withholding love. He refused to sign birthday cards Lori bought, and went to the trouble of expressly denying having anything to do with the gesture. He made no effort to give me a wedding gift, other than allowing his name to be attached to a generic biscuit jar his wife picked out. He even missed the rehearsal dinner the night before. Despite me begging him to be there to see the slide show he was featured in, he refused to arrange his flexible work schedule to fit it in. *What did I expect?*

At one point, I spelled out what it was I wanted from him. I said I wanted him to show he cared about me once in a while. I said I wanted him to reach out and check in every now and then, maybe ask how my life was going.

"I don't even treat my wife like that," he told me.

Derek has always been really smart, quick-witted, and sharp. He loves to debate, but he's stubborn and drives his point through like a battering ram. Proud of his hard-knock education, he's quick to mock college-educated idiots with their bleeding hearts and greedy tax schemes. There's only one way of seeing things, and that's his. However, he's always had a sweet, tender side. For all his faults, he loves my parents and has stood by them through thick and thin. He even took in my uncle's grandson as his own and raised him to be the man he is today. That was the kind of affection I hoped would one day turn my way.

It never happened. In fact, I made things worse by constantly pining away for his attention. By the time things fell apart with Matt, Derek had no trouble picking sides. According to him, there were certain laws that had to be followed. Family was family, so I needed to suck it up and get over it. It didn't matter how I felt or what happened; I just needed to get in line. When

I didn't, he was through with me. I guess family was family, except when it came to me.

A couple years after my niece passed, we were at my uncle's funeral. My relationship with my family was hanging by a thread and the tension was thick. After a couple beers, Derek started carrying on about me. Some family friends convinced me to sit down with him to talk things over. Even my husband thought it would be good to put the past behind us. I relented, hoping that maybe things would be different this time.

For two hours, he lambasted me while slamming back beers, reciting a litany of unforgivable sins I had purportedly committed. I was the golden child. I was selfish and spiteful. I was to blame for whatever happened with Matt, no matter what the circumstances were. I destroyed our family. It went on and on. My husband was shocked at his unbridled rage but tried to reason with him by pointing out where he was blaming me for things that were clearly not my fault (like causing people to get sick by wishing ill upon them, as if I had supernatural abilities that warranted burning me in the town square.)

Despite my apologies to him and Matt, painfully offered after years of feeling like the wronged party, he still refused to see me as anything other than an evil mastermind intent upon dismantling all that was good in the world. It didn't matter what I said or did because I was not a human being in his eyes. I was a mythical creature, an unsympathetic stand-in for wickedness, the scapegoat for all his pain.

The next morning, I pleaded with him and my parents to somehow work through our problems. They sat there in perfect silence as I urged them to figure out how to move forward, how to find the love again. I prodded my dad, but he could only say, with palpable resignation, that looking at Derek was like looking in a mirror. My mom flitted in and out, sputtering angry remarks over her shoulder but refusing my plea to actually participate in the conversation. Derek's wife, Lori, having talked my ear off for an hour and a half about how worried she was about my brother, suddenly had no feelings to share.

Derek stared off into space with his arms crossed until the very end when he sneered, "How arrogant you are to want other people to change."

Knowing all that, I shouldn't have been surprised by his response when I told him about my abuse. And yet, I was.

I don't even remember why I felt the need to bring him into the whole situation, except for the fact that I was addicted to my family. Plus, Derek lived near my parents and was probably already knee-deep in it. In our family, news of drama traveled quickly, though everyone swore they weren't the ones to tell. I suppose I held out some childish hope that he would finally rush in as my savior on a white horse in shining armor, to rescue me from my misery. I also knew that I could engage him in some kind of conversation, one-sided or not, and I needed more external input to counter the limited thoughts that ricocheted around my head like a pinball.

When he answered the phone, my legs went weak and a cold sweat swept over me. The familiar tingle of electricity rushed through my bloodstream as the sound of his casually pleasant greeting smacked my ears with purposeful disregard. In that one seemingly innocuous word—*hello*—he conveyed a treatise worth of sentiment. He knew why I was calling. Whether the knowledge had been rolling around in his head for hours or years, he knew the source of my pain and had anticipated the conversation that was about to happen. He prepared for it, selecting his affect as a strategy in order to convey—without the culpability of words—that whatever I was about to say had no impact on the world order. It was just an average Tuesday, and as such, there was no need to answer the phone with anything more than a neutral—if not forcibly pleasant—salutation.

When I heard him say, "hello," all the words I prepared ahead of time got sucked into the balloon inflating in my throat.

"Do you know what happened to me?" I asked him.

"I didn't know then and I don't know now."

His words knocked the wind out of me. "What do you mean you don't know now? I'm telling you now, so you know now." I was crying and getting more hysterical by the minute.

He flatly told me to calm down, not in a patronizing tone but one tinged with gentleness. Sensing a crack in his armor, I rammed through it with my cry for help.

Through my tears, I erupted. "I can't calm down," I told him. "You have no idea what this is like."

"Yes, I do. It happened to me."

"What?!" I let out an unexpected, blood-curdling scream. This news hit me like a nuclear explosion, forcibly repelling me across the room and onto my butt. I couldn't fully process what he had said or what it meant—or why I reacted so gutturally to it.

"Dad?" I asked.

"No!" he exclaimed. "It was Jack, Grandma's husband."

I was dumbfounded. I lost the capacity to think as memories of Jack sitting on the couch with me, watching movies late at night, seeped into my consciousness. Then I wondered why Derek let him come around years after he moved out, knowing what he was capable of doing. For a moment, I hoped that Jack was the one in my memories. It would have been better to remember him, instead of my dad.

Questions shot out of my mouth, one after the other. "Did you tell Mom and Dad? What did they say? Wait ... why didn't you tell them?"

"Why would I?"

I couldn't imagine holding back that kind of information for all these years. It's not like they would have sided with Jack against my brother. My mom's distaste for the man was settled, especially after he failed to tell her that Grandma Iris was sick. I wondered if maybe Derek was embarrassed. I imagined a strong, stubborn soldier's humiliation must have been ten times worse than my own, which burned like a million bee stings. Maybe his military training taught him to tough it out.

Then I remembered him running away from home as a teenager, and the panic attacks he started having a couple of years earlier. I began wondering if these events were dots that connected to being abused—just as my life's seemingly unrelated twists and turns were beginning to form into the spokes of a wheel sprouting from one central base. Was he holding onto this trauma still? Was I the first person he told?

For a moment, I thought we would bond over this unwanted experience. Maybe the fact that he had been impacted by abuse would make him sympathetic to me. He had suffered the same trauma. Although it occurred under different circumstances, it was the same wound. He might be the only person who could actually understand what I was going through ... maybe this would be the key to unlocking our relationship.

As my mind grasped at these unlikely possibilities like a drunk staggering around in search of his keys, I heard Derek nonchalantly mention that he told our parents about his abuse the other night. My mind sobered up quickly. Just as I assumed, my revelations had sparked a discussion among the three of them, confirming that he did, in fact, know everything before he answered the phone. I can't imagine how that conversation unfurled—with shouts of indignation at such unbelievable accusations or with whispers of shock and sorrow over my perceived betrayal? Either way, at some point my brother decided it was a good time to reveal the abuse he experienced.

This disclosure—a truth bomb decades in the making—was delivered with a tone usually reserved for inconsequential pleasantries like, "oh, and by the way" and "please pass the butter." His cool inflection and apathetic tone rang disingenuous to me, not because he lacked conviction in his emotional indifference, which he definitely had, but because most human beings have feelings about being harmed or knowing that people they love have been harmed. Prison inmates, as a whole, react quite passionately to the subject of childhood sexual abuse, yet my brother was unmoved at not only the fact that I was abused, but that he was.

He refused to feel any empathy or compassion as I cried, offering me nothing, other than a few words to minimize my reactions and deflect my questions. His avoidance made me come unglued, desperate to pull some bit of truth from him. We went in circles as I tried to understand his callous, evasive reaction to my pain, which made me feel like I was cross-examining a witness at trial. Even though my brain was sharp, parsing out inconsistencies and piecing together facts, I could feel my sanity unraveling like a spool of thread with every lie.

"I never said that," Derek said.

"Yes, you did. You wrote it in an email. I can show it to you."

"Well, if I said it, I meant it," he insisted.

He refuted everything that came out of my mouth, undermining my words, my memories, my truth. And he did it with thinly veiled disdain. It's strange to think that he spent decades fully aware of the fact that he had been abused, choosing to downplay and ignore the impact of that wrong, and I spent decades completely unaware of being abused, but flew into a firestorm of anger and pain once I knew. I wonder if my reaction, being so different than his, threatened his way of handling his own trauma. I also wonder if he couldn't allow my truth in because it threatened the pedestal he put my parents on, the one I had only recently destroyed. Whatever his reasons, he went to great lengths to eliminate me and my truth.

Finally, having said everything I could think to say (which wasn't much, considering my head was spinning), I let the silence hang between us. I should have known this was how he would react. He never gave me any reasons to think he would be any different. It was only my childish delusion that made me think he would finally show up for me. I wasn't a princess and he wasn't my brave knight. Seconds ticked by before he spoke again.

"They're only human," he told me.

And all I could think was, *What about me? Aren't I human too?*

# Twenty-Four

Having confronted both my parents and Derek, there was no turning back. My world had permanently changed, and not for the better. I didn't gain the clarity and validation I hoped would enable me to feel less crazy. In fact, their attempts to purposefully cloud things further made me feel even crazier. To make matters worse, they refused to offer any compassion or kindness as I screamed and sobbed over the phone. I had no idea what I expected from them, but it certainly wasn't that.

Their betrayal and rejection pulsed in my veins like a drug, making me jumpy, paranoid, and edgy. It made me self-destruct, blinding me to reason, forcing me to run after what I thought would end my suffering—my family.

I suppose the right thing to do would have been to leave them alone, to wean myself from their toxicity. However, like an addictive narcotic, the painful feelings placed inside me had a life of their own. They ratcheted up, up, up as the minutes and hours and days passed. I was beside myself, unable to soothe my nerves. Before long, I went running toward my family in search of some relief, convinced they were the only ones who could take away my pain. After all, they were the ones who put it there.

After leaving several voicemails pleading and begging and screaming, I wrote an angry email telling them that they owed me the truth. I was their daughter, for God's sake. I wrote that I would do anything I needed to do in order to heal from this, including pressing charges. (I had no intention of pressing charges and wasn't sure I even could, but I knew that would get their attention and make them deal with me.) I couldn't withstand being ostracized, shut out, discarded. It ate away at me like acid on my skin.

I waited for a response, but nothing came. My husband, desperate to pull me out of my rut, dragged me out to get something to eat for our anniversary. I tried to enjoy our time together, a brief reprieve from trying to deal with my insane emotions while being a good mother to our kids, but I was a wet mop. The pain was all-consuming and my feeble—although well-intended— attempts to act otherwise didn't fool Will. Our evening was off to a rocky start, but a start nonetheless, when I checked to see if the babysitter had texted and noticed an email from my dad.

The paragraph was short, staccato. My eyes glanced over his words, but the sight of his name sent my body into a panic. My synapses weren't firing; connections weren't connecting. The words got lost somewhere between my eyes and my brain's comprehension center. I handed the phone to my husband, who read it to himself before helping me digest it. In a few short sentences, Dad said he was sorry and that I was right about everything. Then he wrote that he would plead guilty if I pressed charges.

The restaurant and its patrons suddenly seemed surreal. My husband was just outside my bubble of existence. I was floating above myself, watching as I read and reread the email. I was confused, conflicted.

As difficult as it was to absorb those words, it was even harder to process them. My body, as usual, went tingly and then numb. My heart thudded in my chest, flooding my face with hot blood as the familiar wave of nausea and light-headedness rushed over me. I wrestled with my body's instincts, determined to mind-over-matter myself into a state of stability, yet thoughts kept rushing in and threatening to overturn me. *You were right about everything. I'll plead guilty if you press charges.*

We left the restaurant, and on the way home, I decided I had to call my dad. I felt compelled to talk things through with him, convinced that was the next right thing to do. I'm not sure how I imagined the phone call going or if I considered that at all, but I strongly felt we needed to put it all out there. Lay it all on the table, like puzzle pieces begging to be flipped over and sorted by color and shape. That way I could start putting things together and making sense of it.

I closed my bedroom door, flopped on my bed, and dialed. My hands were shaking, my voice was quivering, and I wasn't sure I could remain conscious. When the phone started ringing, I thought I would throw up.

*Ring. Ring. Ring.*

"Y-ello?"

When I heard his voice, I lost my nerve. I lost sight of why I had called in the first place, panicking as I searched my brain for words—any words, but preferably words that would stop my lip from trembling. I'm not sure what words ultimately fell out of my mouth, but I think I thanked him for his email and then told him that it meant a lot to me. Then I think I asked if we could talk about it.

Years later, my son got really sick and had to stay in the hospital for several days. I wrote him a story about his health scare so that he could process that experience more easily by reading about the brave boy he was as he endured all those procedures. Looking back, I think I wanted my dad to do the same for me. I didn't know it at the time, but I wanted him to fill in the gaps so that I could catalogue these experiences and file them away, rather than letting them float like ghosts around my head.

In a foolish, subconscious attempt to make sense of myself, I asked him my questions of when and why and how. I'm not sure what—if any—details would have satisfied me. I just needed to talk about it, bring it out of my internal world and into the physical where I could observe it as real. He immediately became evasive. He didn't want to talk about it. As unrealistic as it was, I really needed him to offer me something, so I persisted. Seconds into the call, he began to aggressively deny everything.

"I don't remember," he said.

"What do you mean you don't remember?"

His voice became agitated, angry. "I. Don't. Remember."

I was baffled. Why did he write that he was sorry if he didn't remember what he was sorry for? Why did he say I was right if he didn't remember? My inner self began to disintegrate into grains of sand while my hardened exterior pushed forward on autopilot. My legal training took over, guiding me through a series of questions bent on uncovering a bit of truth.

"Were you drunk? Did you black out? Is that why you don't remember?" I hurled questions at him.

"I don't know. I don't remember."

My dad should've been crying and apologizing. He should've been begging me to forgive him, asking me what he could do to make it better. He should've been showering me with care and concern. Instead, he was getting more and more upset as I lobbed questions at him. I could feel his temper rising, bringing mine up with it.

I couldn't believe he would mess with my mind like this. Why would he have emailed me that he was sorry and then snidely rebuke me? I reeled from the whiplash effect of my feelings that swirled around me like a cloud of dust and debris stirred up by a hurricane. Uselessly, I tried to steady myself, tried to make it all stop. And then, in an instant and without warning, it abruptly ceased.

My head cleared out the static, leaving behind a pristine silence. It wasn't eerie or troubled, at least not at first. It was peaceful. In that pregnant pause, my fitfulness gave way to a tenuous curiosity. I leaned into the silence, but my ear jerked away from the receiver when I heard a woman's voice break through it. I strained to make out the hushed whispers, floating through the phone with increasing clarity. It was my mother, spoon-feeding my father words she wanted him to say.

I listened carefully to be sure I heard it correctly. She continued on, unaware that I could hear her coaching him. I wasn't aware of her presence until then, but my gut told me she had been an active participant for some time. Always my father's publicist, she couldn't resist puppeteering the phone call, forcing him to take back the one seemingly honest sentiment he had offered. She was forcing him to take back the truth I so desperately needed to hear.

When this realization settled into my consciousness, I erupted like a volcano and began screaming and cursing at both of them. I unleashed a torrent of words I never thought I was capable of uttering, swearing I would never speak to them ever again. Anger had been a difficult emotion for me to feel, let alone express, for most of my life and suddenly I was overtaken by it. Rage is too small a word to describe what I felt.

Incensed, I screamed through the phone until my voice grew hoarse.

"I'm your daughter! How could you do this to me!? You will never come near me or my children ever again!" I railed at them.

And then it was over.

# Twenty-Five

That conversation with my father felt like a wildfire that was raging out of control, scorching everything in its path. My entire body pulsed with red-hot adrenaline, electric currents moving through me with alarming speed. The intensity of what occurred sent me into a frenzied spiral. I recounted the conversation to my husband, alternating between bursts of outrage and crying spells, until I was too worn out to go on. Then I slept.

During the days that followed, I was too depleted to do anything more than the bare minimum. I floated through my days—making lunches, pretending to eat play-do ravioli, and walking around the block alongside two kids on scooters. I put a smile on my face and offered hallow niceties to neighbors, then slipped into a distant fog resembling a coma as soon as I was free of obligations. I stumbled through life in this haze, safely removed from the impact of what had just happened.

As the days went on, without any word from my family, the haze began to slowly clear. As my faculties returned, the details of what had happened came into view. The torment of my memories returning, my blind, insatiable need for the truth, my mom's sweet voicemails followed by insults, my dad's admission over email, my brother's dismissive tone, me screaming through the phone at them—it all rattled around inside my head, randomly smacking against different emotional buttons. I went from angry to sad to confused, and it was hard to keep up.

My mind, ever eager to make sense of things, kept reliving that conversation and those that came before it. Did I really just accuse my dad of abusing me? Did my dad really write that he'd plead guilty? Did my mom really say she didn't like me? Did my brother really not care after having been abused himself? What possessed me to kick this hornet's nest in the first place?

I went over everything in my head, again and again. It just didn't make sense. I was raised by a loving family who would do anything for me, except they abused me and covered it up, and when I told them I remembered, they didn't seem to care. It came down to two opposite conclusions. Either my entire framework, the foundation I had built my existence upon, was a fraud; or my foundation was as rock-solid as I had thought, and I just deliberately demolished it. In either event, I was left sitting in a charred, desolate reality with only a few embers of rage still blazing, surveying the devastation. Regardless of how I viewed things, everything I thought I knew, everything I thought I was, was no more.

# Twenty-Six

That explosive phone call was the last time I heard my dad's voice and the last time I confronted him about the abuse. I often wonder if we had been able to talk openly, maybe we could have moved past the trauma and reclaimed some kind of connection. In my mind, truth was the way out of the awful place we were in. It wouldn't have fixed everything, but at least we would have had a shot.

During that phone call, however, my mother wouldn't allow things to be repaired. She wouldn't allow the truth to come out, not after guarding it like an attack dog her whole life. Not only was she protecting her husband, whom she loved, from the consequences of his actions, but she was protecting herself. My mom's maternal instincts to protect her family were fully engaged, but as always, I was outside that inner sanctum.

I still wonder what my dad was thinking. I wonder what he actually felt for me when he wrote what he did in that email, and what he felt when he took it all back. I wonder if he truly didn't remember what he did, or if that was just the defense strategy my mom created. I wonder whether he thought he was protecting himself, my mom, or the rest of the family. Maybe he was just trying to save himself by taking the coward's way out, completely unconcerned with what that would do to me. I'll never know.

I guess it's not surprising since my dad's always been a mystery to me. His demeaner's quiet and unassuming, his personality so painfully shy it's often mistaken for rudeness, yet just beneath the surface, seemingly trapped under years of forced responsibility, lurked a boyish playfulness begging to be set free.

My dad was the one who built a bright-yellow speedboat and then pulled my brothers behind it on skis and a wakeboard. Before I was born and during my first couple years, weekends were spent dragging the boat behind their truck camper to the lake where they would camp. They would stay up late into the night, laughing and drinking and telling stories. My dad invited everyone along, including my mom's siblings and anyone else who wanted to join in the fun.

My dad was an incredibly generous man. When my brothers and I were in high school, he paid for school trips and musical instruments and made sure we all had a working car to drive once we turned sixteen. When I went to college, he bought me my very own computer so I didn't have to use the computer lab on campus. He also made sure I had a television so that I could watch the weather in case a nor'easter came through and I needed to be prepared.

He was the one who took us to Disneyland, making us stand in line for the Matterhorn for as many hours as it took to get on the ride. I remember sailing along the Pirates of the Caribbean, his favorite ride, with him giddily smiling the whole way through. On our way out, he would do his best salty pirate impression of "dead men tell no tales." During those trips, he introduced me to my lifelong love affair with churros and made sure we took in the fireworks show at night. To this day, I can't watch fireworks at Disneyland without bursting into tears.

As we grew into adults, he took us and our families on vacations to the lake and to the snow. His favorite destination was Lake Tahoe, where he never failed to drag us out to the Ponderosa for a pancake breakfast. He paid for our whole family, which had grown to include my brother's families, to stay in a cabin for a week during winter and summer vacations.

Dad kept this vulnerable boyishness under wraps in ordinary life. Day in and day out, he was a working man. He woke up to a cup of black coffee, dressed in slacks and a button-up shirt, and headed out the door until dinner. He came home, quiet and drained from the world's incessant demands, and we settled into a night of television. It was then when I sensed his sorrow the most. Sunk into himself, his eyes fixed to the screen, there was no trace of the fun-loving dad I longed for. Other than a puff of laughter or a "huh" in response to my questions, he was gone—relieved, I think, to detach from the stress and strife of the daily grind.

My dad wasn't much of a conversationalist (except when he was drinking), contributing only a few words—and even then, usually at my mother's prodding. She had a way of inciting him to respond, sometimes angrily, if he withdrew too far inside himself. After a couple drinks, his tongue loosened and revealed a little more of his personality.

At first, the alcohol was a welcome lubricant. My dad relaxed and became lively, emboldened with liquid courage. He would say what he thought about a subject, even engage in a debate with my brothers over some topic or another. Sometimes he would reminisce about living in Alaska or a classic car he once owned, or maybe tell a story about my brother getting his car stuck in the mud at make-out point. I loved seeing him come to life in those moments. Of course, the drinks kept coming, and my dad would end up going in one of two directions.

Sometimes, he would allow his sadness to surface, reliving terrible moments of the past as tears streamed down his face, Samantha's name on the tip of his tongue. As a child, this was one of the ways I knew my dad's permanent sadness was intertwined with her loss. As an adult, it was how he made me stop asking for more from him. How could he give me anything when he already gave it all to her? She was gone, and so was his ability to feel love and joy.

After Uncle George passed, I remember trying to comfort him. I was afraid another death in the family, especially after losing my niece, was too much for him. When he began slipping into the quicksand of losing Samantha, I tried to pull him out by reminding him that I was still here and I needed a dad still. He snapped back at me, "You don't know what it's like to lose someone!"

Having lost my grandmas, my aunt, my uncles, my niece, my ex-boyfriend, and my high school friend by the time I was in my twenties, he couldn't have been more wrong, but he saw only his pain, his loss. My feelings of grief were so irrelevant; it was as if I had never experienced them at all. Watching him wrestle with his grief, however, I recalled kneeling next to Samantha's grave as my dad meticulously trimmed the grass around the edges and lovingly polished her stone. Unable to imagine losing a child, I forgave him.

Other times the alcohol would make him belligerent. He would stubbornly lecture about something until he couldn't string words together. One night, he cornered my husband.

"You better not have any skeletons in your closet," he told Will. "I'm telling you. Never have skeletons in your closet. One day, someone will open the door and find them and you don't want that. You need to listen to me on this. I mean it. Keep your nose clean."

This belligerence was better than when, in the early years, he became violent. I was very young during most of that time, so my memories—while emotionally charged—aren't vivid enough to recount. The few familial anecdotes I have to substantiate that point are all I have to make sense of my own recollections, which are vague and frightening.

My dad struggled in the workplace, feeling inadequate without a college degree. He went through several layoffs, each one chipping away a bit of his pride. I think that's what fueled his ambitions for me. He wanted me to be recession-proof. He and my mom had spent too many years worrying about money, and he didn't want that for his kids.

Once I was grown, my parents were tired of the constant threat of unemployment and decided it was time to try something different. Owning a bed-and-breakfast was more of my mom's idea, but my dad needed a change and they found a place in the hills of North Carolina. When I first saw the place, I knew my dad had found his childhood dream. Set up high, overlooking a creek and a barn filled with horses and goats, it was the perfect place for my dad to feel like his childhood hero Davy Crockett.

The first time we visited them at their new place was in the summer after law school. I remember thinking that my dad looked younger and happier than I had ever seen him. He cracked jokes and smiled the whole time, a startling change that was both awkward and endearing. He had an actual bounce in his step. A burden had been lifted off his shoulders, and the effect was magical. Even with the stress of running a small business in a state entirely foreign to him, he was at peace among those green trees.

One night, he dragged Will and me to a roadside firework stand where he bought a ton of explosives, all of which were far bigger and more dangerous than the sparklers I remembered as a child. He proudly emptied them out of his truck, tickled to have upset my mother's nerves, and set them up in the riding arena. After dinner, we sat on the front porch, dangling our legs over the brown-eyed Susans, and watched with wonder as my dad lit up the night sky for us.

That's the last time I remember our relationship being good. We had always struggled, but up until then, we managed to make it work. I loved my dad, and deep down, I knew he loved me—even if he was terrible at showing it. My mom used to say, "Still waters run deep," and I think that was true for my dad. After that summer, though, my niece got sick, and everything started unraveling, disintegrating so fast I couldn't keep up. After the way our connection went up in flames, burning down everything in its path, it's strangely comforting to look back to moments in time like that one and know that we once shared something untarnished and pure.

# Twenty-Seven

Riddled with what I now knew to be post-traumatic stress and trauma brain, I shut down for a while after that phone call with my dad. It was too much to take in all at once. I felt like I had been blown into millions of tiny pieces, and the pieces of me were floating around in space. I was a nonentity, a speck of stardust. My physical body showed up for life, but the rest of me checked into a celestial retreat.

I tried to pick up the pieces of my psyche, insistent on rebuilding my life, but it was pointless. The very foundation of my being had been shattered. I couldn't form myself into a functioning human, let alone put together thoughts and sentences. I didn't know what I believed, what I thought, or what I should do. Who was I? What had I experienced? Questions I had once thought absurd to even contemplate, the luxurious ponderings of philosophers, were suddenly extremely important. I needed answers because the answers to these questions were the building blocks of my foundation—a foundation that had crumbled.

I wanted to comfort myself. I wanted to reassure myself that I truly was the same person I was a year ago, that I was just discovering something new about myself, a tidbit of knowledge that would update my self-perception. I envisioned it like changing my style, trading in my suits and heels for a comfy pair of jeans and a sweater. Although I was undergoing a makeover, I assured myself I was still the same on the inside.

But it wasn't true. I was changing on the inside, at a cellular level. These memories hadn't just inserted an uncomfortable truth into my consciousness, a truth that necessarily altered my perceptions, it forced me to reevaluate every relationship, every decision, and every moment in time. My entire life had been filtered through my delusion, and now that it was gone, everything not only looked and felt different—it *was* different.

It was too overwhelming to look directly at the bullseye of my abuse and my family's reaction, so I started at the edges. I sorted through thousands of old pictures and reread my old diaries. I flipped through the pages of school yearbooks, and I rummaged through overstuffed memory boxes. As I revisited my past, without filters, I felt my way through old assumptions about who I was.

The first assumption I tackled was my lack of domesticity. It was well known that I was not great at cooking, cleaning, crafting, or anything in that arena. I just didn't inherit that gene. It was okay, however, because I was headed to college so that I could earn enough money to have someone else do all that for me. If I was going to have a character flaw, that wasn't the worst one to have. This is how my family viewed me, and consequently, how I viewed myself.

Except, it wasn't an accurate perception. I thought back to my first year of college and how I came home and cooked the entire holiday dinner as a gift to my mom. I thought about begging her to teach me how to crochet her famous slippers, finally getting her to pass on one basic stitch, and using that one stitch to crochet a full-size blanket for my aunt. I pestered her to show me how to work a sewing machine, then taught myself how to make blankets and baby clothes.

I never actually learned to cook, but as a newlywed, I set about learning how. I read through Betty Crocker books and culinary blogs, figuring things out as I went. It took me years to put together a handful of go-to recipes, but I did it. I was proud of being able to nurture my family with food. Plus, in a family of good cooks, I wanted to be able to hold my own.

When I looked back at my life—the meals I cooked, the cookies I baked, the decorations I selected, the crafts I made, the scrapbooks I created, the holiday traditions I started—I couldn't understand why my family thought I was so bad at these things. Then I remembered the artichoke dip. It was a recipe so foolproof that it pleased all my friends and colleagues when I brought it to gatherings. But the one time I brought it to my family, my domestic goddess of a mother managed to "accidentally" burn it to a crisp by cooking it three times longer than instructed—even though she allegedly followed my directions perfectly—and then served it up for my brothers, who had a good long laugh about my incompetence.

From an objective stand point, I wasn't as inept as they told me I was at cooking or crafting or anything else. Uprooting this one assumption set off a domino effect, knocking over more and more assumptions I never questioned before. It was like wiping off layers of caked-on dirt from the surface of a colored tile, slowly revealing a hidden mosaic. I started to see that I was someone entirely different from the person they saw, the person they told me I was.

Then something occurred to me. If they were deceiving me about small, seemingly insignificant things like my domesticity, what else could they be deceiving me about? I thought I wasn't very smart, at least not when compared to my brother, but I graduated at the top of my class in high school, college, and law school. I sat for three different state bar examinations and passed each one the first time. While I worked hard, effort could only take a person so far. I had been gifted with enough intelligence to achieve these honors, but with every success, I felt like an imposter. I feared that one day everyone would discover what my family already knew—that I really wasn't smart.

As I turned over every stone of my self-perception, I began cobbling together a more accurate understanding of who I really was. I threw out old notions and adopted more evidence-based conclusions as to my true self. I wandered back in time, reading through my old journals and listening to long-lost albums, looking for discarded clues to my identity. As I sifted through pictures and mementoes, my younger self opened my eyes to the raw experience of those bygone times, stripped of my family's propaganda.

As I submerged myself in the past, allowing my heart the freedom to explore, I began to come back into my body, to reattach to the world around me, and I stopped feeling like a dust particle swirling about. With every piece of my soul I retrieved and possessed, I grew stronger. My ramshackle foundation had crumbled, but I was rebuilding. Slowly.

I meticulously rebuilt my foundation, piece by piece, but I wouldn't go near the abuse or my family's reaction to it. It was too dangerous. My interactions with my family were just too confusing, too unclear, for anyone to make sense of them. My mom's whispers on the phone. My dad's admission, then immediate denial. Derek's disregard. The complete silence from everyone else. Anytime my thoughts brushed against these events, I shut down. Either the pain, the confusion, or the disbelief prevented me from dealing with it. And yet, these moments returned to my consciousness again and again, begging for attention.

My psyche worked hard to prevent me from facing the truth my memories told, and the pain that truth ushered in, but my body refused to live a lie any longer. My body went rogue, subjecting me to spontaneous bleeding and somatic re-experiencing. When my mind tried to stop it from happening, my body responded with massive anxiety that was debilitating. Shame, unworthiness, and disgust flooded me at the slightest provocation. As much as I really wanted to ignore what was happening, it was clear my body was going to make me face it.

I knew I had been abused for certain. My memories were clear about that fact, even though I didn't have supreme confidence in my recollection of the exact details. I had recalled the approximate age I was, the person on top of me, the rooms I was in, and my mother's voice screeching in the background. However, I didn't trust these memories. I felt I needed crystal clear and irrefutable specifics in order to believe what I knew to be true.

I didn't want to trust them because if I was right, then something really horrible happened to me at the hands of my own family. The family I loved, the family I depended on to love and protect me, had harmed me greatly. And they didn't seem to care.

# Twenty-Eight

Delusion, as helpful as it can be, is dangerous if not outgrown. It's a temporary fix, like a rope tying a sapling to a stake so that it will grow straight. If left too long, it strangles the very tree it was meant to help grow beyond its support. My mom is a cautionary tale about what can happen when you hold onto delusion too long.

My mom has always subscribed to the "fake it until you make it" mantra. She put one foot in front of the other and aimed toward a better life for herself and her children. As much as she wanted to grow beyond her beginnings, she was loyal. Her love for her family—and her fear—kept her tethered to them no matter how their lives diverged. She did so many wonderful things for them over the years, settling into the role of saintly big sister and basking in the loveliness of being needed.

Maintaining this bond required a purposeful avoidance of the demons beckoning to her. If she faced the darkness in her own childhood, it would have shaken her foundation the way it did mine—and *that* would have shaken everyone else's foundation. My mother's role as the unreproachable caretaker made her a pillar of stability in her family and gave her a sense of purpose. Anything that contradicted or undermined this role was a threat and therefore could not be allowed.

When she and my father lost their way after my sister's death, they became violent to both each other and their children. They raged and forgot, raged and forgot, going around and around in a cycle of pain they couldn't stop. Then one line was crossed. Then many lines were crossed. My brother ran away, my innocence was decimated, and a host of other tragedies—quickly forgotten—occurred.

These moments accumulated like snowflakes, burying my mother in a reality she could not bear to accept; they betrayed her understanding of the world, of herself. They did not reflect what she believed to be true, so she deluded herself and everyone else into believing that they had not occurred—or if they had, they weren't all that bad. She was still the perfect mother, the kind and giving nurturer. The truth was malleable, adaptable to her needs at any moment. That was how my mother survived.

After my memories shook loose, I couldn't follow that same path of delusion any longer. There was nothing to hold onto anymore, not even a Christmas card or a text I could read into as evidence of a deeper bond. I couldn't pretend that things were alright, not after remembering, and certainly not after the way they responded.

I felt completely abandoned and alone. Even my husband's love, as pure and lasting as it was, could not take away the pain. My world, my person, had been shattered into pieces, and I was beside myself with grief and hopelessness and pain. No matter how big I smiled or how nicely I dressed, I couldn't make myself believe I was going to survive.

I told no one about what I was going through. Some mixture of embarrassment, pride, and loyalty kept me from opening up to anyone. The disgrace of having been discarded by my dysfunctional family was bad enough, but incest brought another level of shame that was insurmountable. In a world where incest was a pornographic fetish, where people joked about and celebrated pedophiles being beaten and killed, where the elite were permitted to traffic young children for sex without consequence, who would understand my situation? As far as I was concerned, no one.

I was isolated with my struggle. To make matters worse, there was no medication, no self-care program, no healing tactic strong enough to dull the agony that persisted. To believe my memories was to lose everything—my family, my identity, my childhood—but not believing my memories threatened my sanity and tortured my body. I lost either way, and I lost bigtime. I felt trapped with no way out of the endless suffering and came close to ending my life because it seemed like the only way out. I never attempted it, but I came dangerously close.

My family's silence was killing me. It wasn't just that they didn't address the issue; it was that they didn't address me at all. I had ceased to exist to them. I was no longer a living, breathing person on the planet. I had become as invisible as I always feared I was.

Not knowing what else to do and feeling like my survival depended upon her acknowledging my existence, I called my mom. I asked if we could talk.

"Not if you're going to get angry," she said.

I swallowed my emotions, held my tongue, and struggled to express myself in a calm, polite manner. My voice shook and cracked, but I pushed on. "Do you love me?" I asked her.

"Of course I do. You're my shining star, my beautiful daughter."

"If that's true, then how could you let this happen?" I asked her. "You knew."

"I'm not going to get in the middle. It's between you and your father," she said.

"But you're my mother," I pleaded with her. "You know I'm hurting, but you've done nothing."

"I thought it would be best to give you some space. You were so angry and I didn't want to make it worse."

We talked for almost an hour; I chased her down with my questions, and she ran from them. I wanted her to tell me that all of this was a misunderstanding and that she and the rest of my family really loved me. But I wanted the truth more. She grew weary of me, but I persisted. The more I pressed her for answers, the more the truth exposed itself. In her avoidance, her half answers, her distractions, her defensiveness, her lies, she told the truth by not telling it. Then, in just a few short words, she gave me the honesty I needed.

"Can't we all just stay in our denial?"

In retrospect, I know I wanted to say yes. I wanted to put all of this horrible mess back into the dark recesses of my mind, call it a nightmare, and then refuse to acknowledge it again. I wanted to go back in time to when I believed my mother loved me, when I thought she told the truth. I would have done anything in that moment to rewind time, but it was too late.

"No, Mom. We can't all stay in denial because your denial hurts me. It makes me want to die."

Her delusion, the same delusion that helped her survive, was killing me. It was what put me in danger in the first place. Her and my dad and Derek's denial, after all I had been through, made me doubt my own experiences, hate my rational and justifiable responses to it, and loathe my whole being. Her delusion made me confused, lost, and ashamed. It made me wrong no matter what I did. It made me give up on myself and my life.

Yet in my own delusion, I wanted nothing more than for my mom to wrap her arms around me. Whether she told me the truth or not, I wished that she could have made me feel her love during that call. If she had expressed any true, genuine feeling for me in that conversation, who knows what might have happened next. If she had told me the truth, I probably could have forgiven the unforgiveable. But she didn't do any of those things.

I now realize that my mother is not what she appears. She is a façade, afraid of her own substance and intent upon rewriting her history at all costs. Her delusion, helpful and necessary as it was at one point, morphed into something sinister and destructive. It gave her a false sense of relief, distracting her from doing the work necessary to create something solid and lasting. And it allowed her to hurt me. Knowing all that, I'm glad my delusion bubble burst.

# Twenty-Nine

After that call with my mom, I vowed to end all contact with my family, again, although it was an unnecessary resolution considering we weren't really in contact and nobody wanted to reach out to me. Still. I had to draw the line to keep myself from crossing it.

Reason told me it was the right thing to do, but reason did not comfort me. Someone would inevitably ask about my family—innocent questions that most people wouldn't blink an eye at answering: *Where do your parents live? Do you have any siblings? Are you traveling to see family for the holidays? Can't Grandma and Grandpa babysit? Does she get her blue eyes from your side of the family? Who is your emergency contact? Are your folks coming to the grandparent breakfast at school? Why not?* And just like that, I would be face-to-face with the void my family had left in my life. Brushing up against the unbearable pain of having been so worthless, so inconsequential that people could abuse and discard me without giving it a second thought (except to blame me) was too much.

The problem was that separating from my family left too

many unanswered questions for the rest of my life. Traditions and age-old assumptions were suspect, a relic from a period of time that no longer seemed reliable. Parenting strategies, learned by osmosis, had to be reconsidered. Inherited traits were viewed skeptically and sometimes discarded. To make matters worse, I spent my days with little children who were curious about their relatives ... and I had not the slightest idea what to tell them.

In my anguish, I said so many angry things. I swore that I would never let my parents near me or my children ever again. I think I told them to go to hell. Their betrayal opened up my anger at them, and their continued silence made it hard to contain. Years of suppressed feelings gushed out of me like an unattended fire hose as a rage I had never known erupted inside me. Red-hot anger overcame me and seethed out of my pores; I could not keep it inside. I yelled and screamed at my mom and dad and Derek, outraged and indignant at their betrayal. I behaved badly.

But I had so many reasons to be angry. My father had acknowledged the abuse and apologized, even saying he would plead guilty to criminal charges ... and then he took it back. He said he couldn't remember if he had done it. How could he have violated me this way and not hit his knees begging me for forgiveness? Derek said my parents were only human and blamed me for being angry without bothering to concern himself with my well-being. Matt never once spoke to me about it. Not once. Lori, having recently divorced Derek, swore allegiance to my parents and avoided my calls. Auntie May assured me, unprompted, that whatever happened, my mom didn't know about it. The rest of my family remained silent, with the exception of my niece who told me that even if I had been abused, "It doesn't affect a person *that much*." Worst of all, not one of them ever asked if I was okay.

I bounced from one overwhelming experience to another, unable to steady myself. I would melt into a puddle of shame at least five times a day, my face flushing as my body did its best to melt into the ground beneath me. Then I would feel my tears welling up while doing homework with my kids or watching them play, a dam of emotion threatening to burst forth without warning. Sometimes I would feel a rush of rage rise up, eager to be turned loose at the slightest provocation, but fear would silence it into submission and render me paralyzed, pulsing with useless anxiety. I couldn't remember anything, and I constantly lost my train of thought, forcing me to drop out of conversations rather than admit my scatterbrained glitch.

It was hard to live like this. Sometimes I would pour a glass of wine, then another, and another, waiting for the delicious numbing sensation to trickle through me, a beautiful elixir for the ruthless combination of anxiety and dread I couldn't seem to shake. The relief was short-lived, but real. I would inhale deeply, finally free from the agony for a moment. It was then that I understood why my parents drank.

But then I would put the bottle back on the shelf, reminding myself that I would not wander down that path no matter how bad things got. I wouldn't turn to alcohol and drugs, like so many in my family had done, because I knew the destruction that would follow for those who loved me, having witnessed it firsthand.

Sometimes I would be driving, alone in my grief, wondering

if fate would help me escape by launching my car into the center divider, or perhaps a tree. Maybe a simple jerk of the wheel would be enough to let the Universe know I needed a way out. I'd catch myself having these thoughts and pull over, admonishing myself. I was a wife and a mother. They needed me, even if I didn't need myself. I had to find a way to be safe and survive so that—if nothing else—they would never have to know the same pain of being abandoned by their own mother. I would not allow yet another generation to suffer that same wound.

Through all of it, my husband stood by my side. He didn't have to hold my hand as I waded through the worst suffering of my life, but he did. Over and over again, he braced the storm with me, showing me unconditional love, even though no one would have blamed him for quitting us. Not even me. To leave him after all of that would have broken his heart, and I couldn't do that, yet I had no idea how to survive what was happening to me. I was in over my head, completely drowning in emotions I could hardly tolerate. My body was releasing all kinds of terror, operating as an independent agent most of the time. I was confused about who I was, where I came from, and whether or not God cared.

During the dark moments, I thought about how my life would have been different if the people in my life chose to be strong and shoulder their burdens, rather than allowing themselves to collapse beneath the weight of them. I thought about how much pain I would have been spared if my family had faced their heartbreak, rather than stuffing it down until it spewed out in horrifying ways. I imagined what our lives would have been like if they had fought harder for me.

My life then became about stopping the cycles of destruction that had plagued my family for generations. It became about doing better for my children and sparing them from ever knowing the pain I was feeling. It became about letting the pain end with me.

# Thirty

I've often thought about how I would feel if death snuck in like a thief in the night and stole someone away from me. It was the yardstick I used to measure my own decisions. If, God forbid, something happened to my parents, would I be able to live with myself? Even as a young child, I would revise angry diary entries to reflect that I really did love my family—just in case I died and they found the mean things I said about them.

Despite this lifelong way of thinking, when my father first fell ill, I was not prepared. I had not healed nearly enough. In fact, I felt like my heart had been ripped out of my chest and placed in my own hands, still bloody and pulsing. I was raging at the injustice of what had been done to me, outraged at their denial. I was holding out for something to change, having exhausted any possibility of changing it myself.

The Universe didn't seem to care that I wasn't ready. A couple years after I became estranged from my family, I received a message from Derek over social media. He told me our father had been in the hospital for several days and his condition was pretty bad. I didn't know what to do.

My father's egregious disregard for my being in those early moments, moments acted out in an explosive fit of his own unprocessed emotion, changed the course of my entire life. His abuse inflicted me with a virus that compromised my nervous system, warped my self-perception, and insulated me from a healthy connection with others. It fractured my psyche and severed my connection with my innermost self. His crime against me was devastating, and I hated him for the permanent damage he did. I really hated him.

As if the act itself wasn't bad enough, I blamed him for all the hurts that piled up afterwards. My dad was in the eye of my life's storm, his seemingly harmless presence at the center of the destructive forces of my family. One word from him might have altered the way my family rallied against me, but he withheld it. He never stuck up for me, never intervened on my behalf.

I thought it was because he was powerless, broken down by crippling depression and sorrowful rage, and too malleable to my mother's will. I suppose he could have withdrawn from me as a form of penitence or denial, but that left me feeling cast aside, as if I wasn't good enough for his attention. For me, it didn't matter. All I ever wanted was for him to rise above it all and show up for me.

He showed up every now and then, and when he did, it meant everything. I remember having a falling out with my mom and Matt. My dad found me in the garage, fuming with indignation and shame. He offered a conciliatory smile and put his arms around me. My rigid frame collapsed into him and I bawled.

"Sometimes you just need to let them know where you're coming from," he told me.

I'll never forget that moment. I hardly understood what he meant at the time, but I felt his love for me. Just like every time he videotaped my performances or beamed at my report card, I could feel that he was genuinely proud of me. When I visited him at his office, every co-worker knew who I was and fawned over me like a celebrity, and then when he came to my daughter's birthday tea party, he was the one who donned a ridiculous paper crown so he could fit in with the rest of the ladies in their wide-brimmed hats. When my dad did show up for me, it was real.

These moments of genuine concern, few and far between as they were, made it impossible to stop loving him entirely. Unlike the rest of my family, he never purposely cut me down or undermined me. He never set me up to be the butt of a joke or actively tried to make me feel bad like everyone else did. Although he was distant and detached, I never doubted his love for me when we did connect. I suppose that's why, despite his abuse of me, I still loved him.

Many people would reduce my father to a monster, arguing that what he did made him less than human. I think it's easier to dismiss his humanity than to reflect upon the potential for evil that exists in every human soul. Since the beginning of time, people have been committing all kinds of horrible, atrocious crimes against one another. Wrestling with evil is probably one of the most human things we do, other than loving. My father wrestled with his own capacity for evil and many times he lost the battle, but many times he did not. I know my father committed a monstrous crime, but he isn't a monster.

I know that because I saw the good in him. Although I've

often wondered if I invented it, I know I didn't. My dad was a generous, kind man who worked hard his whole life to give his children a great start in life. That's the truth. It was because of the good I saw in my dad that I was willing to do just about anything to salvage a connection to him. I think, more often than not, that all the reasons that keep children, as well as adults, stuck in dysfunctional, unacceptable situations are born out of love. It's a noble thing to love like a child—self-destructive at times, but noble.

Of course, I couldn't dismiss the pain and destruction he brought to my life. Just because I refused to see him as a monster and discount his whole being because of his failures, didn't mean I let him off the hook. It didn't mean I wasn't furious and hateful. I had spent the last several years picking up the pieces of my life and I was keenly aware of who shattered it.

As these thoughts swarmed my overloaded mind, I considered how I should respond to the news of his illness. Beyond my own heart's calling, I wondered what my obligations were in this situation. How was an estranged daughter from an abusive family supposed to handle her abusive father's failing health? If I had been abused by a boyfriend, not a parent, the outcry would be to walk away and never look back. People are not so quick to sever ties with blood, however, and the same harm done at the hands of a parent is quick to be forgiven. We rehabilitate parents and reunify abusive parents with their children, but abusive partners are kicked to the curb. There's a societal expectation that children should stay with their parents, no matter the harm done. I felt that pressure as I tried to figure out the right thing to do.

My family, of course, did not make it easy. My mom never communicated with me. She never picked up the phone to tell me my father had been so sick or that he had been in the hospital for days. I couldn't force myself to call her, knowing she would be ruthless with my emotions and send me over the edge. I couldn't interact with my brothers over the phone without having my guts ripped out and handed back to me. The fact that Derek finally sent a short note was, in their view, more than I deserved. Since my mom had embellished situations in the past in an attempt to lure me into compliance with her wishes, I wasn't sure they would give me the truth anyway.

I feared I didn't have much time to decide. At my husband's suggestion, I resorted to calling the hospital and speaking with a nurse who told me that he was very sick, nonresponsive, and his prognosis was unclear. Knowing that I may not have the chance to say anything at all if I waited any longer, I resolved to reach out. I decided I was going to send my sentiments directly to my father, unwilling to trust that my mom and brothers would give him the message.

I sat down with a pen and paper, scribbling down my thoughts. I wrote down five words, then crossed them out and started over. Then, I did it again. And again. I did this for the better part of an hour, twisting myself into a pretzel. I simply couldn't find the words to express how I felt. It was too complicated to be captured with words. My husband, seeing me struggling, reminded me that I had no obligation to reach out. I didn't need to communicate anything to my dad, unless there was something I wanted him to know.

I thought about the possibility of him leaving this world, his spirit permanently breaking free from its physical form. I imagined the dad I loved being freed of the toxicity, shame, depression, secrets, regret, and numbness that plagued him. He would be free, but what if he looked back at what he left behind? If it was his time, I wanted him to leave this world, and me, in peace. If our roles were reversed, that's what I would have wanted.

So I ordered a bouquet of flowers to be delivered and asked the florist to write a short message: *I love you. I always have, and I always will. And I forgive you.*

Once it was delivered, I called the hospital to ask the nurse to read the note to him out loud. I waited on the phone and listened, then thanked him for helping me. Then I prayed.

Months went by, and I heard nothing. I had no idea what was happening with my father, which was difficult. Having finally learned not to run into the fire of my family, I refused to call or email for an update. I called the hospital a few times, searched for his name online, and then resolved to let go of the situation. I had done all I could.

Finally, three long months later, my father emailed. He thanked me for the flowers, then said he missed me and was happy to put it all behind us. I was dumbfounded. I had fought to overcome my anger and pain, reaching into the depths of my being, in order to offer my forgiveness. I had prayed and worried about his soul, not knowing whether he was alive or dead. After all that, his response to me once he recovered, was to put it all behind us? After three months of fighting to stay alive, contemplating life and death, he didn't offer me the truth or an apology or even an outpouring of love. He offered me the opportunity to relegate my abuse, and the devastation it caused, to the shadows where we could all ignore it. After sending yet another useless email explaining why this was not okay for me, all communication ended again.

Another year went by, another round of birthdays, another holiday season, another New Year's resolution to let go and move on. We had every reason to look forward to the future. My husband and I were closer than ever, and we had three beautiful children who kept us busy. We built sandcastles on the beach, blew bubbles in the bathtub, and mastered the art of living-room forts. After story time and tuck-ins, Will and I would plan our next adventure and dream of what was to come. I suppose it was foolish to think that I could emerge from the battle with my family unscarred, but I did. I really thought I could make a clean break. After all, there was nothing else I could do.

Despite my best efforts, I felt myself slipping into depression. I was floating through life more and more, untethered to the people and places that were supposed to belong to me. When I sensed that I was sinking, I gathered my strength to rally. This usually led to a manic frenzy where I would take on new projects like relocating, moving the kids to new schools, or jumping into a new career path. As I tried to manage my emotions, I wound up creating more disruptions and chaos that resulted in even more emotional stress.

I tried medication, but it made me feel even worse. Therapy, as useful as it was in the early years, wasn't helping. The usual pick-me-ups fell flat, and I was absolutely agitated that anyone thought running, painting, meditating, or bubble baths could cure whatever was wrong with me. Clearly, they were not dealing with the demons I was battling or they would never suggest such a stupid idea as self-care. It was wholly insufficient.

Unfortunately, self-care was my only recourse, so I decided to homestead. We planted a garden and raised some chickens, eager to create our own Garden of Eden. It sounded like a great solution since nature was my greatest solace. I imagined tending my tomatoes, learning how to make jam, and basking in our holistic self-sufficiency. It was my latest tactic to deal with my emotional chaos, and I hoped it would do the trick.

Summer and fall were busy months. Then, around March, I received another message from Derek. I read the first line: *This letter is to inform you of the status of your father.*

His words slapped me across the face, just as he intended. He went on to say that our father was in stage-four congestive heart failure, that he was being intubated, and his prognosis was not good. I had no idea what any of that meant, except that it was bad.

Then I read the rest of his email. He said he understood that I had *anger issues with just about everyone, but now was not the time for hateful communication.* He wrote that it might be a good time for me to reflect and maybe realize that it was my parents who gave me life, raised me to be the person I am—good and bad—and sacrificed so much to provide me with the means and opportunity to have a better life. He reminded me that *there may not be another time to forgive or make peace with your past, but your future will be filled with regret to accompany your anger.*

I thought back to the flowers I sent, the heartfelt words of love and forgiveness I offered. I thought back to my last communication, the email pleading with my dad to acknowledge my pain so that we could move forward, my final attempt to make peace with my past in a way that could include my family. I thought about the years and years of appreciation I showed my parents for all they did for me, my incessant gestures of gratitude, and my life's work of trying to make them proud. Finally seeing my life through my own eyes, I knew his words weren't an honest reflection of me. They were intended to demean me, to reduce me to a puddle of guilt and shame. They were intended to force me back into my role as whipping boy.

Twenty days later, my dad died. I drank a bottle of wine to drown my grief and my confusion. It didn't work. In fact, it only amplified my feelings. My husband called a friend of mine, and together, they walked me around our yard as I cried. Holding me up at the elbows, they marched me in circles underneath the protective night sky. I cried. I yelled. I hyperventilated. At some point, I threw up near the chicken coop. And the next morning, I woke up into a whole new world.

# Thirty-One

No childhood is perfect, no matter how idyllic our hindsight may paint it. It's fraught with growing pains and power struggles and a million little hurts. It's not always as terrible as we remember either. There's always a sweet gesture or a funny inside joke to recall. No matter what goes on in childhood, good and bad moments are doled out, often in uneven measure.

These awkward, sometimes painful years mold us. We are shaped by our earliest experiences, crafted in the same familiar form as our ancestors, a mix of nature and nurture and self-determination. As we grow into ourselves, though, we begin evaluating whether we fit the mold in which we started out and whether we should change it. Sometimes we need to do some tweaking, and sometimes we need to reshape our identities entirely. It's a rite of passage we all go through, the moment we put our stake in the ground and claim our individuality.

When we look back at how we were molded, so much of our perspective depends on the label we choose to define our earliest years. A bad childhood is something to overcome, never to be looked back upon with undeserved nostalgia. A good childhood is something to be treasured, never to be questioned or taken for granted. These black and white categories demand a choice to be made.

I spent years believing I had a wonderful upbringing, then years bemoaning my terrible childhood. I felt a sense of whiplash as I traded one view in for the other, believing there was only one right answer, that it had to be one or the other. Those who raised me also had to fit into the same clean categories. Yet in breaking out of the mold into which I was born, I found it impossible to adhere to such divisive extremes. Choosing one or the other made me feel incomplete.

It's taken a long time to learn to live in the grey area, the foggy in-between where the joy and the pain live side by side, the place where fairy tales are also ghost stories, and where the heroes and the villains are one and the same. This enchanted world of duality and extremes is the place where my dad resides.

It's been years since he passed away, and I still miss my dad. I think of him in the supermarket checkout line whenever I see his favorite Good & Plenty and Baby Ruth candy on display. When my son spots a classic Chevy and starts talking excitedly about how cool it is, I think back to how much my dad loved cars and watching NASCAR races. Every holiday season I walk through memory after memory of him with bittersweet affection. There's never a shortage of reminders.

Yet I hate being reminded of my love for him because it is inextricably tied to my anger and pain. My feelings for my dad are permanently entangled with what he did, and what he failed to do. I can't separate them, so I must learn to find balance between their opposing forces. I can't help but think this is how my parents felt whenever I reminded them of Samantha, bringing to the surface this painful mix of conflicting emotions. I suppose all I can do is honor the fact that I feel both love and hate for a man who did both good and bad as my father, and hope that, in time, it will get easier.

I often look back and wonder what I could have done differently with my dad. I didn't have much time to figure it out, having been "informed" of things so late. I like to think that if I'd had more time, I would have thought of some inspired action. Maybe I would have healed completely and been able to walk into the fray of my family dynamics and stand tall. Whether that's a fantasy or simply a path that never opened for me doesn't matter anymore. The fact is that when my dad passed, I was deeply unstable.

For the better part of six years, I tried to work through things with my family. I did everything I could, even offering unsolicited forgiveness, but every time I came near them, it was a disaster. Their callous disregard and refusal to acknowledge my pain—let alone the trauma they caused—was too much for me. That was why, as my brother pointed out, I somehow plummeted into anger despite my best intentions. Every interaction derailed into something so toxic that I could see no way out of the devastation, allowing suicidal thoughts to creep in. I feared that engaging with my family would send me over the edge.

I couldn't allow that. I had worked too hard to build myself up again. I put everything into being a good mother to my kids, nurturing them and loving them fully. My husband and I had built a life together, a life built on truth and honor and dreams. As I healed from the trauma of my childhood, I found more and more to love about my life. I went hiking, meditated, and painted. I read books and played piano. I laughed and danced and sang. I wished for more. I wanted more. I was more.

Going anywhere near my family blocked all of that out. Every interaction with them left me feeling ashamed, worthless, pathetic, whiny, undeserving, ungrateful, mean, spiteful, petty, and insane. All my good traits were wiped out, as if they never existed. That time I took care of my parents after they got into a head-on collision near my house—even managing to miraculously convince the hospital to waive the hundreds of thousands of dollars in medical bills—was worthless. The work I put into crafting websites for their business, drafting my uncle's will, finding and paying for their attorney—those were all selfishly motivated acts of arrogance, not love. The constant visits, long talks into the night, and sacrifices I made for them were meaningless. Because it came from me, it didn't count. My existence was so awful, so sinful, that no amount of good deeds could overcome it. I was worthless. I was nothing. I should not exist.

That emotional quicksand was dangerous. I needed to figure out a way to be stronger if I was going to put myself into my family's orbit. I needed time to think it through, to come up with some brilliant plan, but there wasn't time. Twenty days wasn't enough.

In the end, all I managed to do was send an email, asking that someone tell my dad that I already said everything I could and that I loved him. I prayed that the angels would deliver my message of love to him in heaven. Then I sent my condolences to my mother, telling her how sorry I was for the loss of her best friend and partner in life.

In all the time his health was declining, my father made no effort to contact me. No email, no card, no phone call. He never showed up on my doorstep, asking to make things right, as I often dreamed he would. He never wrote a letter to be given to me after he passed. He never thought of me, I guess. If he did, he clearly didn't feel the need to let me know.

When I think about my father, my brother's words ring in my ears, and I know he was right. I have regrets to go along with my anger. I regret that my mother never once picked up the phone. I regret that my brother took the opportunity to hurt me when my father passed, rather than heal our family. I regret that my genuine, unprovoked offer of forgiveness—something many survivors are never even able to offer—was forgotten so easily because I couldn't pretend like nothing happened. I regret that my dad left this world with our relationship in shambles. More than anything, I regret that I can't think of a damn thing I could have done to change any of it.

# Thirty-Two

The finality of my father's death was crushing. For so many years, I reasoned that there was always a chance that things would get better, that in time, we would be able to find a way through the trauma. I held onto this hope in the back of my mind, even though I knew better, figuring as long as we were all breathing air on this planet, there was a chance for us. His passing snatched that hope away, and having been deprived of its sustenance, I went into shock.

As the shock slowly wore off, I was flooded with emotions. The complicated grief I felt over my father was hard to wade through, and as I did, all kinds of other emotions exploded like land mines. As painful as it was, I took comfort in the fact that the worst had happened. Everything was in ashes, which meant there was nothing left to burn and, therefore, nothing left for me to try to salvage. Not long after my dad passed away, however, more memories emerged at the edge of my awareness.

I was too fragile, too exhausted, and beyond annoyed at having to deal with any more ugliness. I didn't want to know, so I ignored it ... but the memory persisted. I distracted myself with writing, volunteering, and helping out at school. I focused on gardening, crafts, and working out. I became a mentor and contemplated starting my own nonprofit. I wrote novels and children's books, hoping to create something beautiful and lasting. I wanted to busy myself into happiness and leave my past behind once and for all. I swatted the memory away, like a pesky fly.

Then, out of nowhere, I started dissociating. My mind would go vacant, and I'd slip into a catatonic state, as if my body was paralyzed and my mind was floating away on a cloud somewhere. It was terrifying, especially for my husband who had to revive me by dipping my face in ice water. We hid this insanity from our kids, thinking it would pass the way it did before, but then I fainted on my daughter while we were eating dinner at a restaurant, and I knew I couldn't keep running from it.

I knew whatever it was needed to surface, but I still wouldn't let it. I was at war with this memory, but at some point, I had to admit that the tide had turned in its favor. So I bargained with myself. Perhaps if I let it come out, it would fly away and leave me alone, enabling me to get back to my personal happiness project. Finally, I decided to surrender to its incessant nagging.

In no time, my body flushed with sensations. Images flickered through my sputtering mind, hazy and incomplete. These memories were not the same as before. In these new memories, I was older, around eight, and I knew what was happening to me as it happened. I knew it was wrong. I wasn't numbed out and frozen like before, although the effect was the same. I was trapped by both force and paralysis, my body playing dead while my mind sizzled with shame. In these memories, I was an object of hormonal teenage aggression and curiosity. I was coerced into submitting my own body on demand. And I was at the mercy of my brother Matt.

Once again, I was sent reeling through time and space as the truth made its way into my consciousness. I had come to terms with my dad's abuse, thinking that was the worst possible thing I would ever endure, imagining that I had weathered some of the worst pain imaginable and nothing else could knock me down. Then this memory emerged, completely shattering that notion.

Yet, all at once, everything fell into place. Answers to the unanswered questions I had been grappling with for years seemed to fall into place, one after the other. It was all right in front of me the whole time, but I was missing this critical piece of information that made everything come together. Now that I knew about Matt, my life story began unfolding in a more complete narrative.

I finally understood why I had been so afraid of Matt, why I reacted like an animal whenever he pushed me around. My primal rage was anchored in another time, a time before math homework and piano tutorials and Cheryl. It was anchored in his violation of my entire being.

*… or I'll make your life a living hell.*

That wasn't an idle threat, an exaggerated flexing of his authority over me. It was a warning. He had tormented me my entire life, all with the tacit approval of my parents, but he hadn't just harassed me, wrestled me, or slapped me a few times the way an older brother might. He abused me, and I grew up knowing that he could do it again, without repercussion.

Just like that, I finally understood why—after years of being forced to submit to his demands—I had to take a stand against him when my niece was sick. It was so unlike me to refuse to make nice during such a heart-wrenchingly emotional time. I had given up a paid position during a summer home from college in order to babysit my nephew to help them out. I had swallowed my pride and apologized to them on several occasions to keep the peace. Yet after that episode in the hospital, I could not force myself to sacrifice my dignity to make things right.

I had been sacrificed one too many times, and I simply broke. Like Grandma Iris painting her nails again and again, overburdened with too many years of trauma and strife, something snapped inside me. I hit my limit. No matter how much I loved my niece and regretted the pain her illness spread through my family, I physically could take no more. I could no longer go along with the purposeful sacrifice of my soul, no matter the consequence.

*You WILL be there.*

I was fighting against Matt's arrogant superiority over me, his assumption that my submission to him was a foregone conclusion. I was raging against his smug sense of control over me. In a state of rebellion, I was no longer willing to prostrate myself at his feet out of fear, loyalty, or love. More than that, I was staging an uprising at my family's use of me as a whipping boy. I was putting my stake in the ground, reclaiming my autonomy, and protecting myself ... because no one else would.

*Don't be so dramatic. Just ignore him.*

I remembered the long talks I had with my mom about why Matt made me so crazy. I chastised myself for overreacting to his antics, always flying off the handle. I hated myself for not being able to control my temper, and I asked my mom to help me become a better person. She listened and urged me to get a handle on my out-of-control emotions.

*Do it for me, honey. Do it for the baby.*

My own mother forced me to cower to him, made me stay silent and keep my frustrations and hurts to myself. She sided with him repeatedly, dulling my instinct to ask for help. She told me not to make waves, not to rock the boat. She told me to let it go, to be the bigger person. And when I couldn't, she used my love for her and my family against me

*I'm talking to my son who loves me …*

That night I called, asking about what happened to me as a child, I didn't tell her what I remembered about my dad yet. She didn't know who I thought abused me, or what kind of abuse I was talking about, but she immediately said "nothing happened." Then she had a few drinks and called Matt. Then when I asked her who she was talking to, she threw it in my face that he loved her and I, apparently, didn't.

I thought back to the years and years my parents drank. Despite my dad's violence and abuse of me, they didn't sober up until I was eight. They were still drinking after he abused me, but three years later they stopped, out of the blue. They stopped drinking right around the time Matt was abusing me. Something made them stop. Years earlier, I had asked why they stopped drinking, but nobody would answer me. Aunt May went so far as to lie and say they never drank, an obvious attempt to cloud the issue.

Then I started wondering if Matt knew about what my dad did back then. Did he see it? I can only imagine, based upon my memories, that he heard it. He must have known something since our house wasn't very big. If he did see something, maybe he implicitly thought it was okay. After all, nobody protected me, nobody got help. Everything just went on as usual, so maybe he didn't think there was anything wrong with it. Maybe that's what he told them when he got caught.

My mind spiraled down into anger. Years and years of my mother coming to his side, protecting him. Years and years of my father managing to work things out for the sake of his kids, but not mine. Years and years of Derek punishing me for not making things right with Matt. Meanwhile, everyone knew he mistreated me—and they probably knew he sexually abused me too. My rage swelled.

*You were the one who got mad.*

Of course, I got mad. Any living being on Earth would get mad at such a betrayal.

*Can't we all just stay in our denial?*

If nothing happened to me, like my mom said, what did she need to deny? After all I'd been through with my parents, I couldn't escape the fact that my mom was purposefully blinding herself to my painful reality. Whether she knew all or only some of it, her reactions to my pain made it impossible to believe she had my best interests at heart.

I now saw things from my vantage point, not hers. I trusted what my eyes saw, what my ears heard, and what my feelings showed me. I listened to my own thoughts. Despite my family's voices still yelling at me inside my head, my own voice finally rose above the noise. I didn't need to reach out to them for more of their smoke and mirrors. I wouldn't subject myself to their cruelty anymore, even if it meant I had no chance—however slight—of gaining validation. I knew what I knew.

# Thirty-Three

I've always known that keeping our family together was paramount, especially after the painful separations both sides of my family had endured over the generations. People got hurt when families were split up through death, divorce, and hardship, so breaking up the family was to be avoided at all costs. As I saw in Uncle George's admiration of his own abusive father that cuts and bruises heal faster than the wounds of abandonment. Human beings will suffer a great deal of harm in order to stay connected, to belong. I've done it myself. And the fact of the matter is acknowledging my abuse would have torn my family apart.

Sexual abuse tarnishes everyone it touches. Societal judgment is harsh and unforgiving, reducing child molesters to devilish fiends. Those who look the other way are disgusting criminals, as guilty as the offender. Their children, innocent as they are, have been marked—damaged, sullied, set aside. Nobody wants to take in a child who's been through *that*. It's this secondary wounding that drives children into the shadows, refusing to honor the truth well into adulthood. And so the abuse persists.

My family worked hard their whole lives to build a solid foundation, and bringing the abuse into the light would have ripped through it like a tornado. Rebuilding would have taken a great deal of work, and my family—my mother in particular—would have had to address the cracks in their perfectly crafted public persona to do so.

Worse than that, my family would have lost its sole breadwinner. My mother would have had to fend for herself and her three children alone, and she would have faced losing us to social services. She would have had to go through parent training classes and therapy to work through the problems in our family, which would have required her to face her own childhood traumas, something she was not willing to do. My brothers would have had to face their problems, and everyone would have been dragged through a nasty emotional journey that would have dismantled our family's infrastructure.

Deep down, I think my family didn't believe we could survive such devastation intact, and I'm not sure they were wrong. Having survived so much trauma already, my family was weakened. Choosing to routinely run away from their pain left behind a pretty intense pile of baggage. It was too intimidating to face one of the ugliest crimes against humanity, especially when it meant facing all their other heartaches too. This would have been unbearable given the fact that the trauma I know about is likely only a fraction of what they'd been shouldering. I believe they also felt they had to make a choice between their children, deciding who would carry the burden of what happened. They didn't want to do that, even though in the end, making no choice was a choice against me.

As an outsider, I believe they were paralyzed into indecision and consequently chose denial. The abuse never happened, so there was nothing to do about it. They did the best they could for the whole family. They kept us together, raised me into the person I am today, and did their best to leave the horrific truth in the past. In some ways, this strategy worked. It propelled me into a life of stability and safety, which ultimately enabled me to heal. I can understand how things might have unfolded in this way. But as the lamb offered up in sacrifice, I will never understand how they could forsake me.

I carried the burden of my abuse for a long time without knowing what it was, but like an amputee without an arm, I always knew there was a piece missing. Unlike my family, I couldn't move forward in life as a whole person while a huge piece of my soul was unaccounted for. I constantly searched for it, striving to make sense of myself—and of them—unsure why I was so confused. As painful as it has been to learn the truth of my life, it has given me a sense of wholeness and peace. It's proven to be my Rosetta Stone, the missing piece I needed to unlock an understanding of who I really was.

They didn't just deprive me of my own truth, they persistently weakened my spirit to keep it from coming out. The only way to keep that truth buried was to keep my spirit buried too. I couldn't grow up too brazen or too bold because I would be a constant threat. For me to believe in myself, I would have to believe in what I knew to be true deep down, and they couldn't allow that.

I had to be beaten down enough to stay compliant, to remain loyal. They repeatedly made me doubt myself in every way, disbelieving what my own eyes saw so that I would constantly return to them for clarity. They needed to control me in order to rewrite our history in a way that favored them.

I understand my family more than they know. I may not understand the abuse of a child, but I understand how they devolved into a secretive pit of dysfunction. I understand their faults, and in spite of them, I see their beauty. I can see past their bad decisions to their strengths and goodness. I see them in their totality, and in spite of everything, I love them.

I have spent a lifetime bending over backwards to understand and love the people who hurt and abandoned me, yet they have never once tried to understand me. They never once put themselves in my shoes or tried to grasp my feelings in a situation. Instead, they forced me into one losing battle after another and then blamed me for reacting like any human being would react.

No matter what I did or didn't do, I now see that my family was never going to understand me. Our entire family system was predicated on never understanding me because to do that, they would have had to look at what they did to me and what they continued to do to me for years—and that was out of the question. My family, desperate to avoid the reality they created, crafted a deliberate scheme contrived to keep me down.

Unlike my dissociative denial that was thrust on me as a five-year-old's survival mechanism, they chose their denial. They purposely decided to ignore my trauma and act like it never happened. No matter how family-oriented their intentions may have been at first, they still chose against me. And they didn't just choose against me when I was a small child; they renewed their resolve year after year, adding layer upon layer of hurt to my wounded spirit, without remorse.

My dad betrayed me to my core. The man who was supposed to love and protect me stole my innocence and sentenced me to a life of hypervigilance. He paved the way for Matt to hurt me and didn't protect me. He refused to be accountable for his actions, even when it left me broken. Over and over again, he let me down. Then, as his days on this earth withered away, he left me out in the cold even after I had offered my forgiveness.

Matt tormented me my whole life and never apologized. I spent my entire childhood at the whim of his smug, domineering ways. I once asked him if there was anything he was sorry for—anything he ever did to me that he may have felt some regret for doing—and he couldn't think of one thing, not one unkind word, let alone years of abuse.

My mom knew what my dad did to me and covered it up, and I'm convinced she did the same with Matt. Every time I fought with Matt, my mother suppressed my rage and forced me to submit to him and eventually to his wife. She watched as I slowly deteriorated, and she did nothing to stop it, manipulating my life like a puppeteer with only her interests in mind. Then when I came to her for the truth, she denied me. Worse than that, she was cruel.

Derek, meanwhile, took it as his job to beat me down. He reminded me at every opportunity that I was the family punching bag and that consenting to that role was a requirement of belonging. He sided against me at every opportunity, even without knowing the facts. He never felt compassion or empathy for me, even though our life experiences offered so many similarities and opportunities to connect.

Instead of showing me love and expressing remorse, my family made me feel like I was unworthy and unlovable. They made me feel crazy in every possible way. My family protected their inner sanctum of our unit, but they did it at my cost. Whatever their reasons, they sacrificed me, purposefully, for years.

    Having stumbled through so much of my healing, I knew I couldn't afford to go any further into the wounds of my past. Some wounds are too deep, and some pain is too unrelenting, even for the strongest of souls. Everyone has a limit, and I hit mine when the last wave of memories surfaced. If I dove into that memory or confronted anyone about it, I feared that I would break. I told myself, maybe one day, but not now. I needed to survive and to do that, I had to find a way to move on. I had to leave the past in the past, and hope it would stay there.

# *The Butterfly*

*When the caterpillar has finished reforming into its new adult body, it emerges from the chrysalis totally transformed. At first, its wings are soft and folded against its body, having had to fit within its former shape. After a period of rest, the butterfly pumps blood into its wings to get them working, then within a short span of time, it flaps its wings and takes flight—mastering the art of flying almost immediately.*

# Thirty-Four

Growing increasingly tired over the next several months, I knew I was emotionally exhausted. Grief wears a person down, and after what seemed like an eternity of grieving, I was feeling significantly worn out. On top of that, I was still a mom of three little kids, and that was enough reason to be tired all by itself. Thinking little of it, I downshifted into a slower pace and gave myself time to rest and hoped that would make me feel better.

Weeks and months passed by as I felt myself spiraling down. I was so accustomed to the physio-emotional impact of my trauma that I assumed that was all it was. I tried to rally against it, but there was no use. I was spent. Convinced my trauma was the source of my dwindling energy reserves, I grew angrier and angrier that I seemed to be forever shackled to my past. I doubted I would ever get beyond its impact, and I was discouraged.

Then a lump appeared on my neck.

I called my doctor immediately and went into the office. She listened to my complaints, took a couple tests, and then diagnosed me with mononucleosis. I wasn't sure how I contracted "the kissing disease," but I was happy to hear that it was a normal physical illness that could be treated with antibiotics. Phew. I took the medicine and waited for my swollen lymph node to disappear. When it was still there two weeks later, I told my doctor I had a bad feeling. She assured me everything was probably fine, but she ordered a CT scan just to assuage my worries.

It was a Tuesday night in October when I found out I had cancer. I was fixing dinner, helping with fractions homework, and refereeing a ninja sword fight when my phone rang. Plopping down between two piles of unfolded laundry, I listened as my doctor relayed the results of the CT scan.

"You have a tumor, 12 x 9 x 8 centimeters in size, pressing on your heart and your lungs."

I ran off to my bedroom and closed the door, blocking out the sound of my children. As my doctor talked to me about things I don't remember, I held up a pink ruler to my chest, almost fainting as I realized that twelve centimeters is extremely large when used to describe an unwanted mass growing inside your body. I blundered through our phone call and hung up.

I sat on the edge of my bed and looked up to God, completely bewildered. How could this be happening after everything I had been through? The abuse, the abandonment, the death, the betrayal … hadn't I suffered enough? What was the point to surviving all that trauma if I was going to be taken before I turned forty? Why did God hate me so much?

And why cancer? Cancer had rippled mercilessly through my family. "The big C," as my dad called it, had taken too many lives, diminishing our strength and testing our fortitude. It turned us against ourselves, against God. In my family, it was the worst possible thing that could ever happen, next to losing a child. It was a death sentence, but the kind that was carried out slowly as a form of torture. Cancer, with its disregard for human dignity, was the inspiration for my middle-school research report on euthanasia.

I thought about trying to get Grandma Iris to drink an Ensure shake so that she could get some nutrition, as if I could have stopped her from wasting away before our eyes. I thought about how Grandma Betty succumbed to cancer in a fit of rage. I thought about the years and years Uncle John fought back leukemia, somehow managing to maintain a cheerful disposition until the very end. I thought of Uncle George, Grandpa Del, and my niece who never saw her tenth birthday. Cancer took each and every one of them, slowly and painfully. And now it was happening to me.

The initial shock sent me spiraling into self-pity and helplessness. I just couldn't believe it was happening. I couldn't believe I had cancer. Why me? Why now? Why? Why? Why? Why?

Until cancer, my life had been a tireless campaign to matter. It was about proving myself to my family, and then to others. I felt I had to achieve something of importance to become "somebody." Every goal I set for myself, I reached. I went to college, then to law school. I became a working professional with a retirement plan. I got married, had kids, and bought the big house. I drove a convertible, then a minivan. I rotated through moms' groups, hobby groups, neighborhood friends, and all kinds of cliques. And it was never enough. I was never enough.

I realized that what I had been chasing was not a career, a house, a car, a family, or an invite to a sorority. Whether I wrote a book or founded a nonprofit, I knew it would never give me what I so desperately wanted—unconditional love and acceptance. I wanted the very things that had been denied to me, the things my family withheld.

My therapist often told me that I needed to love myself. She would espouse radical acceptance of all I'd been through and encourage me to parent myself. My husband would gently remind me of everything that was lovable about me, telling me repeatedly that I should see myself the way he saw me. I knew they were right, but I just couldn't seem to do it. After so many years of being treated like a second-class citizen, I believed I was one.

To make matters worse, moving on with my life and being happy seemed to cheapen my survival story. It was somehow tantamount to saying that everything that happened wasn't that big of a deal. How bad could it have been if I was able to build a happy family life and work as a lawyer? My niece would be right in telling me years later that abuse doesn't affect someone *that* much. Former friends would be right when they callously told me that "it made me successful," so I should probably be thankful it happened. Having lived with its effects my whole life, I knew how deep it cut me, and I wasn't about to behave in a way that diminished the devastation.

Plus, my entire person developed within a paradigm predicated on my being worthless, unlovable, and wrong. I had worked my entire life to override these basic tenets of my personality, but I could never fully rid myself of them. They were a part of my cellular makeup, it seemed.

When cancer invaded, however, I instinctually knew that loving myself would be the key to my recovery, and that scared the hell out of me. I knew I had to find the courage and the strength to fight for myself. No one else could do it for me. I had to survive, but I was afraid I wouldn't be able to do that. I was terrified that my spirit was too damaged, too weakened to fight.

At that point, I felt small and insignificant, unsure I could heal from anything, let alone cancer. I was a mere trifling in the grand scheme of things, inconsequential to the Universe. To the extent I still believed in a loving God, I wasn't sure He believed in me.

All of these helpless feelings were hauntingly familiar. I felt them as a fragile little girl, even after my psyche dissociated the cause of them, and I felt them again when my trauma resurfaced as an adult. The fear of annihilation, the injustice, and the powerlessness—they were all the same.

Since I was feeling the same things I did as a child, I decided to do the same thing I had been doing since childhood. I hoped. I hoped that there was a God and that He had a plan for me, one that hopefully didn't include dying of cancer. I hoped that I was strong enough to fight, and that I would be victorious over this awful disease.

With my eyes turned toward hope, I decided to journal. It had always helped me sort through my emotions, and I had so many to sort through that I figured it might help. I found a notebook and flipped it open to find my last entry from a couple months earlier. With my mouth agape, I read what I had written:

*Help. Help. Help. I don't know what else to do. I'm at a complete loss, as if my soul has just died and left my body barely breathing. I don't believe in anything or anyone anymore. I'm disillusioned* beyond what I can bear. I can't find a point or purpose to my life, even though I adore my husband and children. I feel like I am being destroyed, like a thread being pulled from a sweater until it unravels completely. I have no faith, no hope, no energy left. Everything I touch turns to dust, like my entire being is toxic.

 I'm never going to get beyond my pain, which has eaten me up from the inside out. It persists like a cancer, destroying every bit of goodness I fought so hard to maintain. I've tried and tried, but nothing ever works out. I'm constantly chasing after possibilities, but never catching them. I just waste everyone's time, energy, and patience as I desperately try to achieve what has proven impossible for me. And yet, I can't seem to quit, as if my life depends on it. I suppose it does, since without some stupid, impossible task I am delusional enough to attempt—I am left with the cancer.

# Thirty-Five

My own haunting words swept through my body, chilling me to the bone. I had basically predicted my cancer diagnosis, and I had intuitively connected it to my past trauma. It was unbelievable. Spooked, I asked my husband to read my journal entry. He looked at me with wide eyes, equally startled.

I had always thought of what happened to me as a child as a kind of bomb that exploded inside me, shattering my little self into pieces. It not only fractured my mind, but it left festering pockets of knowledge and emotion lodged deep within my flesh. They were always there, waiting for me to discover them and extract them from their deep, recessed hiding places.

Like energetic shrapnel, they had been slowly poisoning me with their unhinged intensity. My body ached to remove them, which was why it constantly brought them to the surface for me to release, but such a task was tedious and slow-going. They could not be extracted with the same haste and carelessness with which they were imposed upon me.

Having been trapped there so long, I now wondered if my body had finally had enough suffering. Perhaps, in all its wisdom, my body heard my call for help and gathered up those broken shards of toxicity into one giant ball in the middle of my chest so that I could finally get rid of it. With the help of others, I could extract that poison once and for all.

As soon as this thought crossed my mind, a voice rose up from deep inside me, a faint whisper too persistent and unrelenting to be ignored. Urgent and aching, it demanded more. More of me, more of life. It urged me to keep going, promising that there was more for me to do and see and be in this life. It refused to let me be defeated, no matter how broken I had become. It told me to find the joy again, to discover what made my life worthwhile, and to believe. It promised me that my life had a purpose, even if I couldn't see it yet.

I wanted to watch my kids grow up, see them establish themselves as adults and be there to cheer them on along the way. I wanted to travel around the world, take in the Northern Lights, and sip cappuccinos in Venice. I wanted to walk my dog through forest trails, take a hot yoga class, and see a million concerts. I wanted to live beside the ocean once again, surrounded by salty breezes and roaring waves. I wanted to laugh until I peed, sleep under the stars, and dance in my kitchen. I wanted to write something real and beautiful. Most of all, I wanted to dream more dreams and chase them with every fiber of my being.

As I imagined all the things I still wanted to experience, I looked back at what I had already accomplished. I went to college and became a lawyer. I lived in a bunch of amazing places and saw all kinds of wonderful sights. I jumped off bridges, learned to ski, tried surfing, went skydiving, and got a tattoo. I met tons of people who taught me so much, and I left my imprint on them. I remembered my good deeds done without fanfare, my endless quest to be a force of good in the world. I saw how smart I was, something I never truly appreciated. I saw my passion, my adventurous spirit, and my unbreakable optimism. I saw my evolution as a parent, the beautiful life I had built, and the legacy of love I was leaving behind me.

I had lived an amazing life, and I had done it all while dragging my trauma around with me. I had pushed beyond my limitations and expanded beyond what I ever thought possible. I healed myself in all the ways I could. My existence, small and insignificant as it seemed, was something to be proud of.

For the first time in my life, I knew that my existence didn't depend upon whether my family—or the rest of the world, for that matter—acknowledged it. My life wasn't predicated on them loving me or liking me. Whether they believed me, approved of me, or even noticed me was irrelevant. It was my life, not theirs. And I wanted it back.

# Thirty-Six

For most of my life, contacting my mother was a compulsive urge I found hard to resist, feeling drawn to her like a moth to a flame. I needed her to see me, to hear me, to know I still existed. For years and years, I looked past every hurt because I needed the most important woman in my life to love me. Like a tiny caterpillar, I truly believed my existence depended on belonging to the leaf I was born on.

*Why don't you care?*
*Of course I care.*
*Then how come you ...* [insert one of a thousand things she did or didn't do]?
Crickets.
*I just wish we could have an honest conversation.*
*I would love to have an honest conversation.*
Crickets.
*How come you don't reach out to me?*
*You were so angry. I wanted to give you space.*
*I never wanted space.*
Crickets.

I didn't tell her about my cancer diagnosis for months. I didn't want her to know. I refused to open myself up to a woman who didn't care whether I lived or died, fearful that doing so might tip the balance in favor of dying. I wanted to live, and I knew I could not tolerate her reaction that would, at best, ring hollow. My love for her made me vulnerable and I needed to protect myself, especially from her.

In the back of my mind, I kept thinking about all the cancer journeys she had been on with other family members. In her family of seven, four had been taken by the disease, and she was the main caregiver for every one of them as their health declined, administering medication and tending to their every need. She was the one who shepherded them through their final days, emotionally conflicted or not.

Thinking about our family's history of cancer made me feel bad about keeping my illness from her. Despite our estrangement, I was hurt that nobody told me how ill my father was before it was too late. It wasn't right to hold back that kind of information. Withholding that kind of thing deprives people of the chance to make things right before it's too late, whether they take that chance or not. I didn't want to be the kind of person who kept secrets, even though I was.

I decided I should tell her, though I had a feeling I was being delusional again, so I let the idea sit for several days before attempting to write an email. Calling was out of the question. I expected to struggle with how to find the right words the way I always did. I expected it to tear me up. This time, however, the words came easily. I said what I felt. I didn't reread it twenty times. I didn't anticipate her reaction or craft my sentiments to try to avoid her predictable responses. I simply told her I was sick, and that I forgave her. I told her I didn't need her to be sorry or tell me the truth anymore, because I had healed myself.

She responded with her usual empty clichés, and that was it. It was the same song and dance, the same superficial act. The fact that I had cancer meant nothing to her. The fact that I could die meant nothing to her. The fact that my kids might lose their mother meant nothing to her. I meant nothing to her, or at least I didn't mean enough to her to overcome all that stood between us.

To my surprise, I realized I had finally accepted that fact—probably for the first time ever. It hurt and it was not okay, but I could move on from it. After years of loving her more than I loved myself, I realized I was finally free. I was free of needing her, or even wanting her. I didn't have to matter to her because I finally mattered to me.

I've heard many people who have been abused as children express that they do not wish to have children. Perhaps if I had truly understood the extent of my mistreatment early on, I would have felt the same way. Since my dissociation was well rooted until after my first two children were born, I'll never know. Still, I'm fairly positive I would have become a mother regardless.

I suppose my higher self knew that children were the answer to my own healing. I would do everything in my power to make sure they grew up safe, seen, and loved, so when I couldn't bring myself to want to get out of bed for me, I got up for them. It was a struggle, but I did it. And I didn't just feed them, dress them, and take them to the park; I showed up for them with my whole heart, broken and bruised as it was.

My kids brought out the best in me. Every day I thought about the kind of mother I had wanted, and I did everything to become that mother for them. I read parenting books, stole ideas from television shows and movies, and mimicked parents I respected. I started traditions and memory books and painted their footprints on the ceiling. I studied parenting experts, but I also studied my kids. I learned what made them tick, what their strengths and weaknesses were, and who they were as humans. I pushed them, coddled them, comforted them, taught them, and exposed them to lots of experiences. I did all I could to give them the childhood they deserved, a mixture of the good parts of my childhood and the childhood I wished I had. Sometimes it wasn't enough, but most of the time it was.

That, I realized, is a gift of my trauma. I was a survivor, battle-tested and proven. I was experienced in trudging up mountains with my eyes turned toward God, determined to maintain my forward momentum. I knew then that I would face my battle with cancer the same way. I would find a way to love my children through it and hold onto my stubborn faith that something good would come from it. And I would be honest with them, focusing not on how far I could fall, but on how far we would climb.

# Thirty-Seven

I waged a battle against cancer for the right to keep living, doing everything in my power to defeat a disease that had plagued my family for generations. I enlisted all kinds of help in my healing journey, from modern medicine to a variety of spiritual practices.

I also listened to that voice that had risen up in me. I walked through cancer on a mission to heal not only my body, but my entire being because I knew, deep down, that cancer was an opportunity to face my greatest demons once and for all, and to finally reclaim my soul.

In between chemotherapy treatments and acupuncture, I took care of myself like I was the most precious creature in the entire world. I lathered my body with incredibly fragrant soaps, singing songs of encouragement to my cells. My husband would peek into the bathroom, grinning, as I got out of the shower, dancing.

"Go body, go body, go! Go body, go body, go!"

I listened to kindhearted strangers guide me through healing affirmations online. I repeated mantras as I did the dishes or lay lifeless on the couch. I took walks—mostly slow, meandering ones—and enjoyed the simple pleasure of feeling the wind against my skin. I fed my body nourishing soups and broths, and I treated myself to bubble baths. I took long, restorative naps.

When I was up to it, I fed my soul too. I sewed a blanket with my daughter and lay inside my sons' forts. I read inspiring books and wrote pages and pages on my laptop. I watched old movies I loved and discovered new films I loved just as much. I taught myself to play songs on the piano, singing along as my fingers played "This Is Me" from *The Greatest Showman* and "Learning to Fly" by Tom Petty. I flipped through travel books, lusting after destinations and making plans to go there as soon as I was better.

Because I was going to get better.

As the chemicals were infused into my body, I visualized tiny warriors going to work on my tumor and all it comprised. I saw them chipping away at it with pickaxes, steadily destroying the enemy inside me. I saw me on the sidelines, hollering and shouting like a fanatical parent at a soccer game.

I spent a long time meditating and praying. In the stillness, I surrendered to fate, but I also argued for more time and begged for mercy. I sunk into the deepest part of my essence, feeling comforted by my own heartbeat and the warmth of my innermost being. As I went inside myself, I felt a peace I had never known before.

One day, while meditating, I recalled a vision I had around the time my memories first surfaced. It came up while I was doing some healing writing, unfolding like some kind of story I learned as a child, or maybe a dream I dreamed time and again.

I saw myself split into two little girls. One little girl was in a long nightgown, clutching a stuffed animal under her arm, nervously pacing. She was alone in a dark, stone hallway and was guarding an enormous locked door. She wasn't able to see what was inside, but I could.

Behind the door was the other little girl—the other me. A Native American man was holding in his arms the little girl, limp and battered, and a young Native American woman stood next to him. He gently laid her on the stone floor and looked protectively over her unconscious body. Then the Native American people left, looking over their shoulders in sorrow just before disappearing.

This vision, or whatever it was, stayed with me for a long time but drifted away over the years. I hadn't thought of it in a while, but as I was meditating between chemotherapy treatments, it came back. Unsure but curious, I allowed myself to bring it to mind.

This time, I saw the same scene unfold, the same familiar characters. On the stone floor I saw my limp body, lifeless and abandoned, and the watchful girl guarding the door. But then something different happened. The pacing little girl turned around to see the enormous door open. Cautiously, she tiptoed inside and knelt down beside the other little girl's limp body. She put her hand on her shoulder, and quite miraculously, the other little girl's eyes flittered opened.

To me, that symbolized the way my soul and my psyche had been split in half. I had been separated from a part of myself that was hidden away for safekeeping. I didn't know if that part of me had died or was dormant, and I had no idea how to unlock the door in order to reach that part of me. I was stuck on the outside, still a child myself, vigilantly protecting this vulnerable aspect of my being for eternity.

In this second vision, though, the door opened for me. I was able to walk through it and find the lost part of myself—and that part was not dead. It was very much alive and eager to reunite.

# Thirty-Eight

Having cancer was a miserable experience altogether. It stripped me down, taking my vitality and my hair. It hurt and ached. It broke my heart. I struggled to take care of myself, let alone my kids, and worried about things I never want to think about again. As a family, we walked through a dark, scary time together, fortified by our love and the belief that we would get through it somehow.

Every day I looked for joy and counted my blessings. I searched for happiness in every nook and cranny of my life, celebrating even the smallest victory. We walked around our neighborhood, looking for sparks of joy—a pinecone, a holly sprig, a happy dog walking by. We created art together and curled up to watch TV under blankets. My voice couldn't read bedtime stories out loud for very long, and sometimes my kids ended up tucking me in if I fell asleep too soon, but we found a way to carry on. At the end of every night, I was grateful for my little family and the time I had with them.

When I was really ill, I thought about writing letters to my children, just in case. I couldn't imagine them getting married or having babies without their mom around, so I figured I would write a few things down for them to read in the future. I wanted them to have a piece of me to carry with them, to know just how much I loved them. But I didn't write any letters. I decided that I was going to be at those events. I was going to make it through cancer and tell them all those things myself. In person.

I soldiered on, hopeful and determined. Then, five months later, in late February, I experienced serious pains in my chest. The doctor sent me to the emergency room for a full work-up, worried that my heart wasn't tolerating the harsh chemotherapy drugs. One of the drugs I was given was known to damage the heart, and I was scared out of my mind. After a few tests, I waited for the results. Finally, the ER doctor came in with a piece of paper in hand.

As I lay on the gurney with a mask over my face, I held my breath. He quickly assured me that my heart was fine and then rambled on about some other matters. I stopped listening after he said my heart was fine, my relief oozing out of me like air escaping a balloon. When he left, however, my husband turned to me in tears.

What I hadn't heard was what the doctor said about my tumor's measurements, so my husband rattled off the numbers he gave, as if I could understand their significance. I stared at him, confused, as he explained to me that those measurements were significantly smaller than the measurements taken when I was diagnosed. In fact, my tumor had shrunk to half the size. I couldn't quite take it in, so my husband broke it down for me.

The chemotherapy was working. The tumor was shrinking. I was healing.

Knowing that the medicine was working infused me with such hope and faith. I was buoyed by this news. I had braced myself for a long haul, preparing to try treatment after treatment until one of them worked. I had made peace with the possibility that I might be fighting for my life for years, but that possibility was irrelevant now. Finding out that I was on the road to getting better made me want to run full speed toward the finish line.

Unfortunately, I couldn't heal any faster. The healing process was long and arduous, even with my uplifted spirits. The treatments were just as awful, and given the wear and tear on my body, I was feeling much worse as time went on. Doubt and fear tried to creep in as my strength waned and my body cried out for respite, but I pushed through. Like a runner in the final few meters, I gave it everything I had.

And somehow, by the grace of a God I thought had abandoned me, and with the help of modern medicine, my body healed completely. I was able to rid myself of that awful disease. In a matter of five months, the tumor that had been the size of a potato disappeared, and there were no signs of any other abnormalities. In less than a year, I was cancer free. I had conquered "the big C."

As I recovered, I began to regain my strength. I experienced the incredible sensation of air filling up my lungs to full capacity, a feeling I had sorely missed. My muscles moved with eagerness, and my stomach craved foods of every kind. As I felt my life force inhabiting my body once again, I overflowed with happiness like never before. But it was more than that.

For the first time in my life, my skin didn't prickle at the slightest fright. Anxiety loosened its grip on my stomach, and shame didn't flush my face whenever someone looked at me funny. My body was not only cancer free, it was also free of so many of the symptoms I had been carrying around since high school.

I've read research tying childhood trauma to chronic illness—cancer, in particular. There are studies about how childhood trauma causes a myriad of physical issues later in life. I'm not sure how to make sense of the science behind it, but I know from experience that my cancer was not just a physical illness. For me, it was so much more.

I fought my cancer battle on many fronts, attacking an enemy that had turned my own body against me, and I won. But I didn't just win the right to keep living. I won back the shattered parts of myself I lost as a child and integrated them into my being once again. After a lifetime of shadowboxing, I put down my gloves. My battle with cancer, as it turned out, was redemptive.

# Thirty-Nine

Life is filled with ordinary miracles, the kind that go unappreciated in the daily bustle of living. Quiet and unassuming, they are patiently waiting to unfurl at just the right moment. Like a butterfly emerging from its chrysalis, miracles come in their own time and on their own terms. More often than not, they emerge through transformation.

The process of transformation is not pretty. It's messy and oftentimes terrifying. It most definitely isn't for the faint of heart, but those who endeavor to bring it about are never disappointed. Not only are they offered the gifts of a rebirth, but for one incredible moment, they are part of the secret plan of creation.

It's crazy to think that a caterpillar undergoes its transformation inside the chrysalis by slowly digesting its own body from the inside out. How nature evolved that creature in such a way that it would have to break itself down completely before reforming into an entirely new being is absolutely astounding. It's part magic and part miracle, a beautiful mystery that is breathtaking to witness.

I wonder if the caterpillar knows how its life will unfold from the beginning. Does it eat through leaves day in and day out, knowing that it will soon dissolve itself and morph into something new? Or does it follow its natural instincts, happily unaware of what will happen next? When it begins creating the chrysalis, does it dread the work to be done, or does it approach it with curiosity? I wonder if, as it begins to digest itself, it doubts the plans the Universe has for it.

For most of my life, I believed I was a caterpillar, that I was meant to crawl on the sweet earthy soil, constantly searching for sustenance and never finding enough of it. I thought I would forever live my life as easy prey, in constant fear of being wiped off the face of the earth. For so many years, I clung to the leaf where I was born. The only thing keeping me going was the instinct to feed myself and grow beyond the skin I was born into.

At various junctures in my life, I could have fallen into irreparable brokenness. Addiction, depression, and suicidal thoughts were just a few of the pitfalls I managed to avoid. Sometimes I was airlifted out of the darkest stretches of desolation and delivered into something better. Other times, I clawed my way out with nothing but pure grit.

When the time came for me to form a chrysalis and dissolve myself into my cellular building blocks, I thought I was over. I couldn't comprehend life beyond the pain of my own internal destruction. Everything I held true disintegrated, leaving me with nothing to hold onto but my own substance. It was dark and lonely, and after a life of fearful fervor, I couldn't imagine why God would have led me to such a terrible place.

Yet I survived that isolation. I endured the demolishment of my being and allowed the rebuilding to occur, inside and out. Although I felt abandoned and frightened and disillusioned beyond anything I thought possible, I surrendered. I allowed the process to unfold with the hope that something good would come of it. And it did.

I've lived a metamorphosis, the kind that dissolved me into primordial goo and rebirthed me as an entirely new being. Parts of me are built from my earlier life, refurbished and reorganized to accommodate my new form, but mostly I am an entirely new human—unrecognizable, even to myself. I have grown and changed in ways that make my earlier life feel unreal. While I was undergoing this massive transformation, I didn't know if I would emerge from that dark time at all. I certainly didn't know that I would come out of it stronger, braver, and happier than I'd ever been.

I've emerged a butterfly of sorts, and my wings are still new. I am learning to rise above the life I have lived up until now and to embrace the endless possibilities all around me, possibilities I couldn't even see from the ground where I once existed. I am growing into my new self, eager and excited to see what will unfold next.

For the first time, I can see that I am an ordinary miracle. I was born with everything I needed inside of me to grow and become more than I thought possible. I know that my existence, however unexpected and perhaps even unfortunate for some, was not a mistake. No one's is.

I'd like to say that my transformation ended like a fairy tale, my beautiful wings taking me over the rainbow, but it didn't— or at least it hasn't yet. I'm still an orphan struggling with some stubborn remnants of my childhood trauma. I'm still missing pieces of my memory; without connections to my past, I'm adrift without an anchor. I'm still a little sad about all I've lost and all I'll never have, and that sorrow persists even when I'm bursting with joy. As Cinderella must know, a blissful "ever after" cannot erase what happened "once upon a time." And I don't think I'd want that anyway.

I have a lot of scars from this life. Some you can see—like the port scar on my chest or the gash on my eyebrow—but others are hidden, like the scar tissue that runs down my throat deep into my chest or my overworked adrenal glands. Some, like sorrow and heartbreak, are invisible to the naked eye. I used to hate my scars, but I don't mind them so much anymore.

My scars remind me of the battles I've fought to be here, battles I have emerged from victoriously. I'm proud of my survival. Even when I could see no way out, I held onto life, to hope, and to the idea of "one day." It may have made me crazy and dysfunctional at times, but it kept me moving forward. No matter how bad things seemed, I never gave up. I never allowed my pain to make me mean and hateful toward others. I never let it turn me bitter and cold. Through all of it, I held onto the best of me.

Without my scars, I wouldn't have anything tangible to show for my valor. There's no medal of honor to recognize my victory in overcoming trauma or cheating death. There's no financial compensation for my suffering. There's not even a loyal group of followers on Instagram to share in the bliss of overcoming the greatest obstacles of my life. I traveled a dark, lonely road, and at the end of it, there weren't a lot of people there to celebrate my achievement. For once, though, that's okay. After a lifetime of longing for external recognition and corroboration, I've learned that the only validation I ever really needed was my own.

My life has tilted the scales in favor of overcoming. I have transmuted pain into hope, hate into love, and fear into strength so that the atrocities I suffered end with me. I have managed to pull off a generational reset, clearing the way for my children and their children to make the most of their lives without first having to crawl out of avoidable devastation.

My children, like all human beings, are sparks of divinity trying to make their way through a world filled with strife. They are a mix of nature and nurture and self-determination, a combination of both good and bad. They have been molded by their earliest experiences, just as I have been, and one day they will look back and decide what is worth carrying into the future and what is worth leaving behind. I hope they take the best of me with them, the way I've taken the best of my family with me.

And one day, when they are faced with some terrible truth or some incomprehensible injustice that makes them want to give up on themselves and the world, I hope they are fortified by knowing my truth. I hope they see that honesty, courage, and strength are qualities we all possess, and sometimes they must be challenged in order to shine. I hope they choose not to let the ugliness of this world defeat them, but instead, rise above it with beauty and grace. Most of all, I hope they see that life, even one as turbulent and painful as mine has been, is always worth living.

After everything I have been through, I truly love my life. I love my body, bruised and battered as it may be from the journey. I love my mind and my heart and every crazy emotion I get to feel, even though I'll probably never make sense of it all.

I love the fact that I get to fall asleep next to my husband and wake up to the sound of my children. I love that I get to feel the sun on my face and the wind at my back as I walk along the ocean. I love smiling at strangers and listening to music and baking cookies and hiking and reading and petting my dog. And I love that I get to dream and create and wonder about all that is yet to be.

I'm grateful my journey isn't over yet. I don't know how many years I will get, or if I will ever totally understand the things that have happened to me. I don't even know if I will do all—or any—of the things I want to do. Like Truman Burbank, I must face a future that is wholly unknown. But I'm free now. I'm free to live this life—this excruciating, beautiful life—on my own terms with full possession of all my pieces.

And somehow, that's enough.

# Acknowledgements

Thank you to all of the people who made this book possible. You know who you are.

www.ingramcontent.com/pod-product-compliance
Lightning Source LLC
Chambersburg PA
CBHW072150100526
44589CB00015B/2170